In Remembrance:
Lindsay Crittenden Dorney-Richard

*"Throughout our quarter-century together,*
*Lindsay was with me every step. Everything I wrote she*
*edited, every presentation she critiqued. Through her,*
*I learned love and joy."*

© 2018 Wilfred E. Richard

Library of Congress Control Number: 2018954388

ISBN 978-0-9967480-5-6

Designed by Harp and Company,
www.harpandcompany.com

Distributed in the US by Casemate Publishers and
around the world by Oxbow Books

IPI Press
Post Office Box 212
Hanover, New Hampshire 03755

The Arctic Studies Center
Department of Anthropology
Natural History Building, MRC 112
The Smithsonian Institution
PO Box 37012
10th and Constitution, NW
Washington, DC 20013-7012

Cover photograph: Uummannaq by air, in summer.
Title page photograph: Uummannaq by air, in winter.
Printed in China

# Between Sea and Glacier:

## Greenland in a Changing World

Wilfred E. Richard

Published by

IPI Press

and

ASC-Smithsonian Institution

# Table of Contents

# Why Greenland?

Family, community, and church shaped my core value system. But, my character as an individual evolved while wandering the hills and forests, throughout the four seasons, near where I was raised in northern New England.

By the time I was 12, I was an avid hiker and by 14, I was a winter camper. In my 20s, my life centered on backpacking and skiing the backcountry of New Hampshire's Presidential Range. This is where I found my soul mates. I could never leave the world of nature for long. Then, in my 50s, I began traveling to the north, by coastal kayak in Labrador, and then further north to trek Canada's Baffin and Ellesmere Islands. That trekking turned into traveling and bivouacking on the ice, and finally to Greenland.

My next stop, beginning about 12 years ago, early in the new millennium, was northwest Greenland, where my wife Lindsay and I found a second home. Having experienced so much of my life through close identification with nature, the naturalness of Greenland—its culture and its people—has become my spiritual place. Through my appreciation for the world of nature and through fellow travelers who are inspired by Gaia, the spirit of the earth, I have found solace. In the Arctic, in Greenland, I have found a place still largely unaffected by the works of man. As they have been for millennia, glaciers and icebergs are simply there, neither manipulated nor replaced. And it is here that the fundamental value of the Greenlandic community model of cooperation transcends that of the aggression inherent to the western-bred economic model of competition.

The people of Greenland possess a robust spirit, born of the land, which speaks to me. At this time of the Age of Man, the Anthropocene, of human-induced climate change, I recognize that a tradition of respect for the land prevails in Greenland. With all the community dependent on the land, a spirit of cooperation has evolved through a melding of Inuit communal culture with Scandinavian social democracy. I write of Greenland, of its culture and people in possession of an existence, which is based on hunter-gatherer knowledge of the land. If we *Homo sapiens* are to successfully control the impact of our species, we need to emulate the ways of the Greenlander, who never went through agricultural or industrial revolutions that defined the earth simply as a commodity to be manipulated to meet our whimsical needs as defined by a market economy. In the images and text that follow, I communicate a 'sense of place' for of a northern place worthy of reflection and emulation.

In 2014, William Fitzhugh and I produced the book *Maine to Greenland: Exploring the Maritime Far Northeast*. In it, two chapters focus on Greenland with the operative word being exploring. The book, which you are now reading, sprung forth from that 2014 publication. Here, I progress from exploration to discovery as a progressive vision of northwest Greenland. Ethnographer Knud Rasmussen and godfather of Inger Knudsen (see below), writes of "discovery and definition as two sides of the same coin." Contrary to those times, of the early 20th century, he did not seek to discover "new poles and passages." Rather, he sought "the discovery of peoples and their connections" (Hastrup 2016, 116). Further, Rasmussen's work "bears on an anthropological argument that knowledge of others is a matter of sociality" (Hastrup 2016, 127; Jackson 1995,119). Finally, Hastrup (2016, 129) offers how Rasmussen was not detached; rather, he offered "friendship and intimacy".

The focus of this book is Uummannaq, a functional Greenlandic community surrounded by a still-pristine geography largely unshaped by our own species. While I am certainly no Rasmussen, my vision is of Uummannaq as a place, a culture, and a people—in Uummannaq as well as elsewhere in Nuuk, Iceland, Canada, and Washington, DC, and also visitors to my home in Maine. If there is a US state with repeated historical connections to Greenland, such as those of polar explorer Robert Peary, nautical explorer Donald MacMillan, artist Rockwell Kent, or current-day adventurer Hodding Carter, it certainly is Maine.

# Preface

This elegant volume, *Between Sea and Glacier: Greenland in a Changing World*, written and photographed by Will Richard, explores a part of the northern world rarely visited by outsiders. Home for more than 4000 years of Inuit ancestors, Uummannaq continues to support a traditional Inuit hunting and fishing lifestyle whose origins trace back to the Siberian Paleolithic, but which today combines a subsistence economy with all of the advantages of the modern world: cell phones, *Facebook*, snowmobiles, drones, and international travel. This portion of West Greenland is known to outsiders primarily for the calving glaciers that export massive amounts of ice from the Greenland ice sheet. Few are aware that this small Arctic village and its surroundings contributed some of the building blocks for Arctic exploration and archaeology, for polar meteorology and geophysics, was a famous destination for 17th and 18th century European whalers, and was the home of some of the first Inuit emissaries (read: 'captives') to be seen in Europe. Uummannaq and the greater Disko Bay region are also a likely location for the most historic meeting ever witnessed since the dawn of humanity, when ivory/walrus hunters from the medieval Norse settlements in southwest Greenland met Asian-derived Dorset or Thule Inuit peoples ending their migrations through Asia and northern North America, bringing human migrations 'full circle' around the globe.

Will Richard is a seasoned traveler who has spent his life searching for knowledge about northern peoples and lands. After extensive travels in Newfoundland, Quebec, Labrador and Baffin and Ellesmere Islands, he finally reached Uummannaq, a town and people that he and his wife, Lindsay, adopted and visited many times. As the relationship with Uummannaq developed and its Polar Institute (UPI) was created, the yearly visits north were reciprocated by Greenlanders visiting in Maine at the Richards' home in Georgetown and in nearby Owl's Head, where Jakobshavn (now Ilulissat)-born Inger Knudsen Holm Morse, goddaughter of Knud Rasmussen, settled with her husband Dr. Edward Morse after meeting on one of Donald MacMillan's Arctic voyages. Will Richard's chance meeting with the Morses at the L.L. Bean store in Freeport, Maine, set off a chain of linkages that are reported in detail in the pages that follow.

Uummannaq is indeed a special place. Its spectacular physical geography dominated by a heart-shaped mountain dramatically announces 'special character'. Scientifically, Uummannaq is known mostly for its archaeology and geophysics. Even though archaeologists have barely scratched the surface of its numerous ancient Inuit settlements, it is famous as the location where Greenland's Inugssuk culture, an Inuit people whose culture included a blend of traditional Thule cultural elements mixed with European materials and objects scavenged from abandoned Norse farms in the 14th and 15th centuries, was discovered. Here Danish archaeologist Therkel Mathiassen (who discovered the Thule Inuit culture while on Knud Rasmussen's Fifth Thule Expedition in Canada in 1921-1924) and the young American archaeology student Frederica de Laguna (destined for fame for her studies of Alaskan Native cultures) documented the first instance of Pre-Colombian European influence on a New World culture, two centuries before a second wave of European contacts began, this time by Dutch whalers. Uummannaq was also the staging point for the first scientific study of the Greenland Ice Cap, a venture led by German geophysicist Alfred Wegener, famous for his prescient continental drift theory and for organizing the first International Polar Year (1881-1883), in which nations around the world sent scientific teams north simultaneously to explore the Arctic in a systematic manner—the first instance of a global science approach. Wegener's death on the expedition in 1930 signaled the perils of conducting science 'on the ice' in the pre-aircraft era.

Uummannaq tells these stories and many others. We learn about the region's geography, animal resources, impacts of climate warming, and the history of its prehistoric and recent Inuit cultures. We make excursions to abandoned mines and ancient Inuit settlements and graves, including the place where the famous Qilakitsoq mummies, now respectfully displayed in the Greenland Museum in Nuuk, were discovered. We visit the small town where American artist Rockwell Kent lived, communed with nature, and painted for several years in the early 1930s. Richard introduces us to the Uummannaq community and its leaders and institutions and describes the work of Børnehjemmet (Children's Home) that has given a new start to some of Greenland's disadvantaged youngsters by rekindling knowledge of Inuit traditions. Greenland's crafts and artists, traditional literature and dance, kayaking, and dog sledging are described. We experience the polar night and how Uummannaq has developed social adaptations including kaffemik, rites of passage, and cultural and national celebrations to blunt the winter twilight and mark seasonal transitions.

In addition to serving as a personal diary and thoughtful introduction to cultural life in a remote Greenland settlement, Richard provides us with food for thought as we contemplate the course ahead for this one village and for the entire world. Inuit have lived here for thousands of years, and during that time experienced many changes in the climate, environment, and animals that sustained them. They met Viking Norsemen, Dutch whalers, and Danish missionaries. The 20th century brought U.S. bases and strategic bombers, then détente, and now rafts of ship-borne tourists and scientists arrive to view and study the rapidly retreating Ilulissat (Jakobshavn) glacier. Climate and environmental changes are not novel to Uummannaqers; they have seen such cycles before, and they survived. But modern cultural changes pose new and perhaps more dangerous risks that may disturb the social and cultural fabric of the town. One key to the future is maintenance of a sustainable fishery and to avoid over-dependence on mining and fossil fuels. Tourism and science are proving beneficial, as are the external contacts exemplified by the historical connections with Maine and visits by the Børnehjemmet children to Maine and the Smithsonian Institution in Washington D.C.

Will's text is accompanied by his own stunning photography that richly amplifies the story of this community perched along a mountain fringe between the Greenland Ice Cap and the sea. His images reveal the gnarled ribs of the earth, the monumental size of Ilulissat icebergs, the excitement of a seal hunt, and the cairn graves of the ancient Inuit. Through his photography we participate in a Lutheran church service and home meals, play with youngsters, and meet Inger Knudsen Holm Morse and Dr. Edward Morse, and Ann Andreasen and René Kristensen of UPI and the Children's Home. Through Will's picture-scapes we experience Uummannaq like it was our own hometown.

There are important messages here if we look and listen carefully to our guide, Will Richard. Mankind would do well to emulate the values exhibited by the village of Uummannaq, where people have lived lightly on bare rock for thousands of years.

*William W. Fitzhugh*
*Director and Curator*
*Smithsonian National Museum of Natural History, Arctic Studies Center, Washington, D.C.*

# Dedication to Inger Knudsen Holm Morse

Central to this story is Inger Knudsen, later to become known by the surname Knudsen-Holm and eventually Knudsen-Morse. Inger touched lives in space and time, from Greenland to Europe and to North America, over nine decades and four generations. To have known Inger is to be indelibly smitten for life.

Some years ago at my annual Christmas exhibit of photos of the north at the L.L. Bean store in Freeport, Maine, Dr. Edward Morse approached and introduced himself as the doctor on the last MacMillan Arctic Expedition. With him was his wife, Inger Knudsen Holm Morse, who was raised in Jakobshavn, then a Danish colony (now Ilulissat), where Inger's father, Aage, had been *Kolonibestyrer* (Manager) of the North Greenland District for the Kingdom of Denmark. Inger was born and raised in Ilulissat when it was still Jakobshavn. As a historical footnote, the name 'Jakobshavn' was bestowed on a heretofore Inuit settlement in the 18th century in honor of Jakob Severin who defeated the Dutch in a sea battle. With the demise of colonialism, the Greenlandic term Ilulissat, 'icebergs', became the town's new name.

The first child of Aage and his wife Else was Inger, born in 1921. Sister Helga followed, then twin brothers Per and Eb, and lastly sister Kirsten; all were born and raised in Jakobshavn. Later the King of Denmark knighted Aage in recognition of his efforts to keep Greenland aligned with the Allies during World War II. Sisters Inger and Helga had godfathers who remained legendary in the Colony of Greenland. Inger's godfather was Knud Rasmussen, an explorer and ethnologist who traveled by dog sledge to Canada and Alaska in 1921–1924, and Helga's was explorer, writer, and anthropologist Peter Freuchen; Uummannaq was part of Aage's North Greenland District, the next town north of Ilulissat, over the Nuussuaq Peninsula (Map 2).

For much of the recent past, the history of this northwestern section of Greenland has been recorded through the observations of the Knudsen, Morse, and Holm families. Inger Knudsen Holm Morse and Edward Morse reminisced through their stories of life in northwestern Greenland. The Knudsen family in the northern reaches of Danish Greenland had established connections with Maine as early as 1934 through the presence of Donald and Miriam MacMillan. Aage made a gift of two puppies to the MacMillans on their boat, the Maine-based *Bowdoin*. As a child, Inger was very much involved with training dogs. By age ten, she had her own dog team. Later, Dr. Morse sailed to the Arctic with MacMillan as ship's surgeon.

For decades, Ed and Inger made their home in Owl's Head, Maine, where Miriam MacMillan was a frequent guest. Yet another caller was Kate Hettasch, otherwise known as 'Labrador Kate' for her nearly 50 years in Nain, Labrador, as a Moravian Missionary and

**The Bowdoin anchored in Jakobshavn Harbor, Greenland**
*Donald MacMillan sailed the Bowdoin from Maine to Greenland on many of its Arctic voyages, which began in the early twentieth century. The Bowdoin continues to sail, including a 1994 trip to Uummannaq and a 2014 voyage to Nova Scotia. Image from Knudsen-Holm family archives used with permission.*

**Aage and Inger Kundsen as their Jakobshavn home is constructed**
*In the early 1920s, almost a century ago, the Knudsen home in Jakobshavn was built. It served as the District Headquarters for Denmark's North Greenland Colonial Manager, Aage Knudsen, father of Inger, who poses with carpenters. Image from Knudsen-Holm family archives used with permission.*

**Knudsen home in the1920s and almost 100 years later**
*The structure has not changed much. It is now a museum, a center point of any trip to Ilulissat. Image from Knudsen-Holm family archives used with permission.*

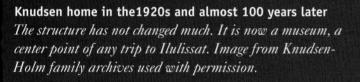

**Inger with her dogs in the 1920s**
*As a child, Inger was as adept at running a dog team, as were most Inuit adults. Image from Knudsen-Holm family archives used with permission.*

**The MacMillans aboard the Bowdoin**
*Donald, the explorer and namesake of Bowdoin College Peary MacMillan Arctic Museum, and Miriam MacMillan stand on the deck of the Bowdoin with two puppies, which Inger had raised. Image from Knudsen-Holm family archives used with permission.*

teacher. In succeeding years, my wife and fellow traveler Lindsay and I cherished our time with Inger and Ed at their home in Owl's Head.

In January of 2010, a day-or-two after we arrived home in Maine from Uummannaq, a phone call came in from René Kristensen in Uummannaq to inform us of Ann Andreasen's birthday. René was organizing a birthday celebration by Internet for the following day. Lindsay and I were already scheduled to be with Inger Knudsen and Ed Morse on that day at their home in Owl's Head; so all four of us together in Maine sent our birthday greetings to Ann. The composition of the birthday card image seemed to be particularly fitting, coming from all of us who are familiar with both Uummannaq and Ilulissat.

Visible in that photo is a painting, *Maliq*, by Emanuel Petersen, over our seated group. Malik—also referred to as Maria—was a domestic helper to Else, Inger's mother, in the house that was Inger's childhood home. That home in Ilulissat is now an art museum containing several works of Danish painter Emanuel Petersen. Petersen's paintings evoke artistic elements of both Rockwell Kent's imposing landscapes and Norman Rockwell's domestic celebrations of daily life. With Owl's Head as our conduit to Uummannaq, we sang 'Happy Birthday' in the spirit of the Greenlandic *kaffemik* celebration (see Chapter 8: Culture) to Ann in Uummannaq.

**From left to right, Will, Lindsay, Inger, and Ed, in Owl's Head, Maine, celebrate Ann Andreasen's birthday in Uummannaq**
*From the sun porch of the Morse home, Inger sends birthday greetings to Ann in Uummannaq. The oil painting of "Maria" in the background is by well-known Danish painter Emanuel Petersen. Maria, a native woman, was the domestic helper in the Knudsen household. What was then the Knudsen home is now the Ilulissat Art Gallery.*

**Both in their ninth decade**
*Inger and Ed stand by a painting that symbolizes much of their lives — sailing ships, the sea, and Arctic ice.*

The Knudsen family home in Ilulissat, always a welcoming place, is just a short walk up the hill from the harbor. I recently enjoyed looking through a book by Inger and Ed, *Growing up in Greenland,* that was published in 2012. It was with delight that I saw that it included an earlier image I had taken of Ed, Inger, and brother Per visiting from Denmark in Owls Head. Inger's family continues to live in Maine. Inger's son Bill, who has his home in Camden, is a tugboat engineer in the waters of New York City. Grandson Max, also of Camden, is a Maine lobsterman. Inger's love of adventure lives on. Inger passed on August 9, 2013. Ed passed three years later on September 30, 2016. This photo of Ed and Inger was made the last time that all four of us were together, in April 2013.

Black and white images contained in this publication, from the Knudsen-Holm family archives, are provided courtesy of Bill Holm, Inger's son. My thanks to Bill Holm for his Greenland-like, magnanimous sharing of the Knudsen-Holm family collection.

**Geometry of the land draws the eye**
*Land and water on a calm day.*

**Arctic Heartbeat**
by Shawn Rumbolt (Metis).
Soapstone and moose antler.
11" high x 10" wide.
St. Anthony, Newfoundland |
Forteau, Labrador. 2001.

# Introducing Uummannaq

Twenty thousand years ago, everyone on earth was a forager [hunter-gatherer]. By five hundred years ago, well under one person in ten still practiced this way of life.... The few survivors are mostly penned into extreme environments that farmers do not want such as the Kalahari Desert and Arctic Circle,...[But, by] the 1980s most hunter-gatherers practiced fossil-fuel-assisted foraging....[m]odern foragers are the products of distinctly modern historical processes, above all European colonialism...

*Ian Morris. Foragers, Farmers and Fossil Fuels: How Human Values Evolve (2015, 28).*

## Author's Introduction

My intent in this book is to introduce the reader to a section of the continent of North America, that remains, even in this day of Google Earth, beyond cognition. This was not always the case. Throughout the nineteenth century, into even the twentieth century, through fishing and whaling, there was some rudimentary awareness of the frozen north and of the 'Eskimo.' Through World War II and the 'polar route' over Greenland, which connected North America to the European theater of war, Americans and Canadians who served in the military gained a greater appreciation of the Arctic and subarctic regions. The Air National Guard flies a segment of this route, from Stratton Air Base in Scotia, New York, to Kangerlussuaq, Greenland, for the National Science Foundation.

When I speak of Greenland, my observations and comments focus in particular on the island of Uummannaq, Greenlandic for the 'heart shaped' mountain that defines the island, and the town of Uummannaq and its surrounding settlements, with a combined population of about 2,300.

With global warming and the dramatic melt rate of Greenland's ice, a pending disaster has spurred a resurgence of interest in Greenland. That interest, however, is encumbered by our often limited comprehension of the geography, culture, and people of Greenland.

There is at least an awareness of the Arctic on the North American continent, which may be reached through either the State of Alaska or the Commonwealth of Canada. We are connected to this part of the Arctic by land and culture. This is not the case with Greenland which can only be reached by air or water. You cannot drive a car to Greenland, and it is a chore to fly there. Until very recently, one flew from North America east to Denmark, then caught a flight west and north to Greenland. That geographical roundabout trip is expensive in terms of dollars, time, and especially patience. Once there, there are no roads between settlements—all the roads are on the coast.

Over the decades, much of my professional life as geographer, anthropologist, and photographer has focused, like a laser, on Nunavut and Greenland. I have a need to pass on to society the substance of what I have observed and learned of the Arctic north; it has become my life mission to share that experience. With *Between Sea and Glacier: Greenland in a Changing World*, I write of life in a particular community, Uummannaq, in that huge island's northwest region, north of the Arctic Circle. As a person who has made it my life to live close to nature, I have found in Uummannaq, and in Greenland, a place, a culture, and a people that aspires to live in companionship with nature. To experience life in Greenland enriches mind, body, and soul.

This book is a testimony to personal ties established over the decades between Greenland, Denmark and Maine through friendships forged with Inger Knudsen Holm Morse, formerly of Jakobshavn, Greenland, and her husband Dr. Edward Morse, once the ship's surgeon on the Bowdoin, which explorer Donald MacMillan commanded on many voyages to Greenland. Our friendship, beginning with a chance meeting at the L.L. Bean store in Freeport, Maine, has continued at Dr. Morse's home in Owl's Head, Maine. With Inger's death in 2013, family records that she had inherited from her parents, Aage and Else, were subsequently passed on to Inger's son Bill Holm. The records include 13 volumes of images. Bill generously offered their use to me, and I have reproduced many here with permission.

I was very fortunate to have the friendship of Kunuunnguaq Fleischer, then a lead researcher for the Government of Greenland. Named after Knud Rasmussen, he was Kunuunnguaq, 'little Knud'. Rasmussen's mother was a Fleischer. Kunuunnguaq introduced us to Ms. Ann Andreasen, Director of Børnehjemmet, the widely respected Children's Home in Uummannaq and Director of the Uummannaq Polar Institute. Ms. Andreasen has created and developed educational and therapeutic activities deeply rooted in Arctic nature and local Greenlandic Inuit culture. Good friend René Kristensen moved from Denmark to Greenland in 2001, at which time he began his career with the Uummannaq Children's Home, specializing in hiking, hunting, fishing, and dog sledging, which we often enjoy together. Without the support of these friends and other colleagues, I would never have had an entrée to Greenland. In the United States, I wish to thank Renee D. Crain, at that time Program Manager, Arctic Research Support, National Science Foundation for arranging Greenland air travel. My thanks also to colleague and friend William Fitzhugh for encouragement and for insightful questions and comments. To my wife, Lindsay, my heart-felt appreciation for continued support of dreams and endeavors.

If you are one who has an appreciation for nature, or even if you do not, here is a book to start your journey–for here is beauty. With climate change, we need to become more aware of cultures that live lightly on the land, as do the people in the communities of Greenland.

With Uummannaq as my focus, I discuss geography, leadership and change, culture, archeology and climatology, economy—traditional and current, climate, and maintenance of a culture.

Floe edge emptiness

## Geography: Greenland – Uummannaq Fjord and the Nuussuaq Peninsula

Geography...is finally knowledge that calls up something in the land we recognize and respond to. It gives us a sense of place and a sense of community. Both are indispensable to a state of well-being, an individual's and a country's.

*Barry Lopez. About This Life: Journeys on the Threshold of Memory (1998, 142).*

Greenland, or Kalaallit Nunaat, as it is known in Greenlandic, is the eastern-most terminus of the indigenous people who migrated over the millennia from Siberia. This section of northwestern Greenland is roughly centered on 70° to 71° north latitude, or about 5° north of the Arctic Circle.

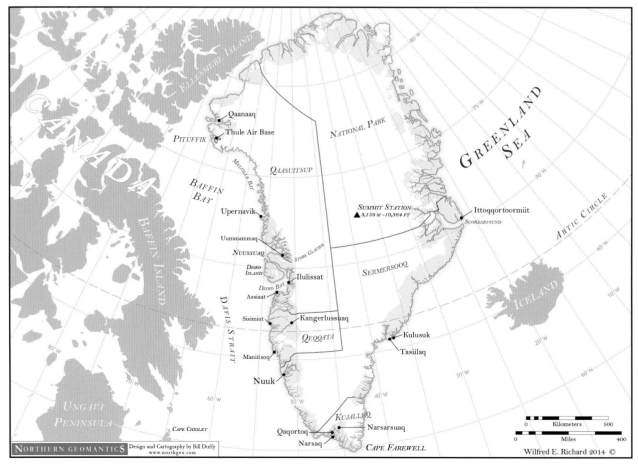

**Map-1:** *Greenland is the central land feature of the Arctic in the Western Hemisphere.*

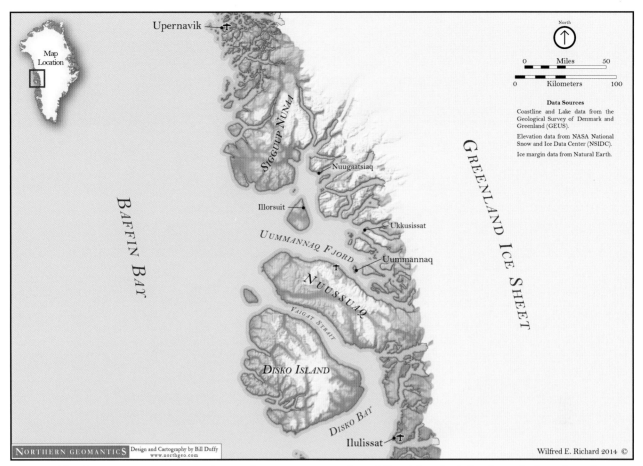

**Map-2:** *Northwest coast represents the northern-most expression of Danish colonial rule and of continued European cultural presence, melded with Inuit culture as 'Greenlandic'.*

Rudyard Kipling, who never set foot either near or above the Arctic Circle quixotically described this part of the planet as "…somewhere on the cool side of the Arctic Circle" (1895, 261). This land is a grand panorama of fossilized whiteness; it remains uncluttered by humans and their works. To appreciate this place and its people requires of the outsider an eager interest to explore, to learn, to become involved. Here there is a sense of place, and a respect for that place and its bounty, a bounty gathered mostly from the sea, but increasingly also from mining, a bounty that has sustained the community.

The primary focus of my story is Uummannaq, with a secondary focus on Ilulissat. Uummannaq, an island, is the municipal center for seven settlements situated around Uummannaq Fjord. Ilulissat is the administrative and economic center for this region. Nuussuaq, which is a peninsula, is shared between Uummannaq and Ilulissat. 'Northwest Greenland' is a geographic expression or classification derived from the Danish colonial period. This region extends north from Ilulissat to Upernavik; these towns were the northern-most Danish colonies in Greenland. Map-1 shows that Greenland extends north from Uummannaq for another 900 miles, reaching 13° further north than the top of Alaska.

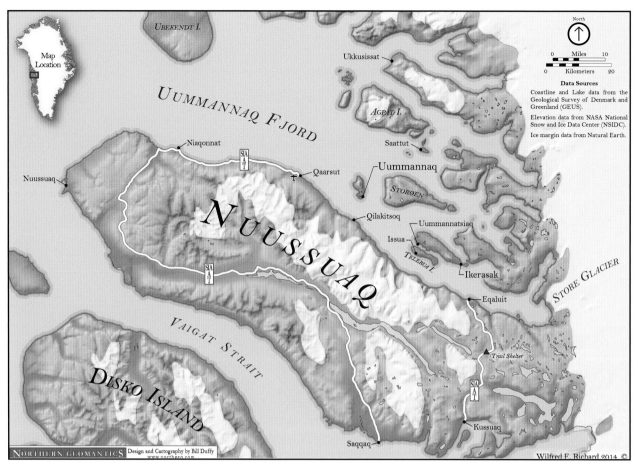

**Map-3:** *Nuussuaq, 'peninsula' in Greenlandic, is the primary land feature, which is shared by Ilulissat and Uummannaq.*

Greenland is the world's largest island, extending from Cape Farewell in the south, which is the same 60° north latitude as Cape Chidley at the northern tip of Labrador, to 83° north latitude. With the exception of a narrow stretch of land (overwhelmingly rock) situated along the coastal circumference of this sub-continental island on which most Greenlanders live, the great mass of Greenland remains covered with ice and snow. Greenland constitutes the northernmost landmass on the planet, extending beyond 83° north latitude. Uummannaq, the geographical focus of this work, is located at slightly more than 70° north latitude, which is slightly further north than Point Barrow, Alaska, the northernmost point in Alaska.

Map projections from a round object (earth) to a flat object (paper) result in distortion. Normally this distortion has been allocated to the Polar Regions. With Mercator being the most common form of projection, distortion has historically been allocated to high latitudes because it was thought there was little value to the area. From the colonial point of view, no one—only a few natives—lived there.

With these map distortions, Greenland appears larger than its actual size, yet this massive island is more than 25 percent of the size of the contiguous 48 states of the United States. Map-1 is designed to show the location of place names that are referenced in this book. As Greenland is largely unknown territory, with place names that are not English in derivation,

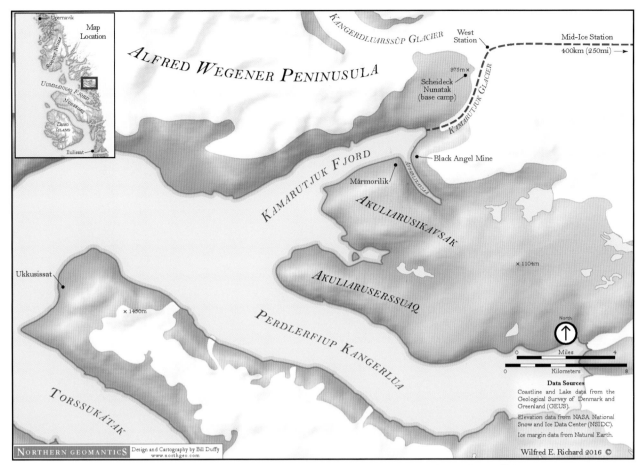

**Map-4:** *Northern Uummannaq Fjord, featuring the Alfred Wegener climatological expedition of 1930 – 1931.*

I suggest that the reader take time to become familiar with place names and relative locations on these maps.

The Mercator projection was first used in the late 16th century. With whaling as important as it became, starting in the 17th century, accurate nautical charts became increasingly more important. More recently, the commercial need for accurate maps has grown with the potential for navigation through the Northwest Passage.

Europeans, 'Norse' (likely Norwegians), first settled Greenland around 1000 AD in the southern region of Cape Farewell and as far north as what is today Greenland's capital, Nuuk. Following the onset of a much colder climate, The Little Ice Age, these colonies died out sometime in the 15th century (The Little Ice Age roughly spanned the period 1300 to 1850, see Fagan 2000.) Then in the early 18th century, Scandinavians returned, but this time it was primarily the Danes who occupied Greenland, as far north as Upernavik. Denmark, Greenland, and the Faroe Islands constitute what is known as the Danish Realm or the Kingdom of Denmark. Greenland has been self-governing since 2009.

Frederika de Laguna (see Chapter 6), a young anthropologist on her way to conduct fieldwork near Upernavik, first saw northwest Greenland in 1929. Dr. de Laguna was enraptured by the penetrating brilliance of Arctic light,

aptly describing what is seen in the image above, as 'Winter Sun Rise'.
The scene she describes in the image that I took eighty-years later, in the
winter of 2009/2010, has changed little:

> *The night hours between 6 P.M. and 6 A.M. are by far the best in the twenty-*
> *four.... I have never seen anything so beautiful as Uummánnaq Fjord*
> *at midnight. ...Over everything is cast a rosy glow.... Greenland is the*
> *most lovely country in the world (1977, 65-66).*

The black and white image on the following page records the town of
Uummannaq, as de Laguna would have seen it in the 1920s. But, the color
image does more justice to the light quality of Arctic winter.

There are currently seven widely scattered settlements, located on nearby
islands and peninsulas, in Uummannaq Fjord. In the recent past there
were perhaps twice that number. Uummannaq is a place, a culture, and a
community, all with an intimate connection to *siku*—the frozen sea. As

**Winter sunrise**
*Even at five degrees north of the Arctic Circle there is still a winter sunrise, which is produced by the refraction of light through ice crystals in the air both above and below the horizon.*

of 2013, the island municipality of Uummannaq had 1,282 residents and its satellite settlements an additional 972 for a Uummannaq Fjord regional total of 2,254 (Statistics Greenland 2013). 'Uummannaq' is a Greenlandic word meaning 'heart-shaped' (that of a seal), signifying the shape of the mountain that dominates the skyline of the Island of Uummannaq, as seen in the front cover. Located about 490 km (300 miles) north of the Arctic Circle, the municipality of Uummannaq is the supply and service center for the surrounding settlements. These areas in Uummannaq Fjord are of necessity glacier-free enough, year-round, to provide sufficient land area for settled communities.

The global electronic media have wrought changes in Greenland. But, my focus here is not so much on change as it is on how our 21st century global culture can benefit from our knowledge of this arctic community. Greenland is a place where cooperation prevails in a culture that lives largely off locally available resources. Thus, I present Greenlandic culture as a model worthy of emulation by our agro-industrial world.

*from top:*

**Town of Uummannaq in 1929**

*This view, from south to north, is toward the islands of Uummannaq Fjord, which lie off the north shore of the Nuussuaq Peninsula. The town of Uummannaq along with islands and scattered peninsula settlements constitute the collective municipality of Uummannaq. The island in foreground is Storøen; in background is Ikerasak. Image from Knudsen-Holm family archives used with permission.*

**A winter's morning**

*This image was captured in the winter of 2009/2010 on a day with four hours of daylight. View is of Nuussuaq Peninsula.*

**Midnight in Uummannaq Fjord**

*Late one night while returning by boat from Qilakitsoq, located on the Nuussuaq Peninsula, we happened across this magnificent iceberg with its massive tunnel. Inger Knudsen tells the story of flying through one of these tunnels with World War I ace German fighter pilot Ernst Udet. While he lived in the region of Uummannaq Fjord in the early 1930s, Rockwell Kent captured the power of such a scene many times in his drawings and paintings.*

Artists and scientists who visit Uummannaq either out of personal interest or who are invited as guests are supported in their professional endeavors in Uummannaq. These visitors are encouraged to contribute their work to the Uummannaq Polar Institute (UPI) so that it is available to other Arctic scholars. For example, visitors collaborate with *Børnehjemmet*, the Children's Home, in such activities as film production and the children's orchestra. Some films, such as *Inuk*, which presents a message of a resilient, adaptive, and self-affirming culture, have been widely viewed in Europe and North America. With the advantage of frequent air travel to Europe, Russia, the Americas, and elsewhere, the people of Uummannaq, who 'learn as they go', largely set their own destiny.

Through the depiction of a rich and fascinating culture, along with the beauty of Greenland, the images and text of this book document an authentic culture that long predates our own agriculturally based system. Otherwise, the term 'culture' is derived in concert with the western tradition of tilling the land; that is, the agricultural revolution, 12,000 years before the present (BP), and of the industrial revolution beginning about 1750 AD during the age of European expansion and colonialism. Here, the term 'culture' refers to ways of life that are applied primarily to those connected to the sea—hunting on its ice and fishing in its waters. In a universal sense, the concept of culture has more relevance as an adaptive mechanism. As a cultural geographer and photographer, I present images of the reality of a people engaged in their daily rounds. This story of Uummannaq is essentially a guide for seekers to the hinterland of northwest Greenland.

Travelers to Uummannaq—as well as elsewhere in Greenland—are not only welcome but are encouraged to extend their stay. This island, with its signature heart-shaped mountain, fjord, and peninsula, is not a mass tourist destination, nor will it ever be. The Uummannaq region is for those curious travelers who delight in being close to a demanding climate and a friendly culture, with a minimum of tourist-support amenities, i.e., the trappings made to lure today's upscale travel market.

As for much of the Arctic, Uummannaq is caught in the chaos of change. Change can be painful—family breakdown, migration for economic reasons, lack of skills for a market-based economy. But change can reveal new knowledge to apply to shifting paradigms. To this end, there are two proactive institutions in Uummannaq that monitor change and recommend policies and programs to adapt. These two agents are *Børnehjemmet*, the Children's Home, which was established by the colonial government to render assistance to children who are deemed to be at risk (For further discussion, see Chapter 3-Agents of Change), and the Uummannaq Polar Institute (UPI). The UPI was established

*... At [the] beginning of [the] International Polar Year 2005 – 2007 as an educational and research institute through which to maintain Greenlandic culture. This endeavor requires a balance between hard-won traditional ways and modifications wrought by western modernization and climate change.*

Government of Greenland. Founding Statement. Uummannaq Polar Institute, 2007.

Much of the text and many of the images in this book have been made possible by support from these two institutions, whose mission is to encourage and support change. Examples contained herein capture both modern and traditional culture, archaeology and climatology, tourism, and climate change, and are celebrations of continuity and adaptation. All are directed within one context, which is to prepare for Greenland's future. Here, I offer the fundamental value of local, dynamic leadership that addresses change through creative solutions. For example, the exposure of children to the world outside Greenland is encouraged. Many musicians and artists from Europe have visited Greenland to teach and perform for the town's youth. In turn, these youth have gone forth as musicians themselves, to perform in such places as the Vatican and the Court of the Queen of Denmark.

Through the Children's Home and UPI, young Greenlanders become the next generation of leaders who will go forth to serve as transmitters and receptors of cultural knowledge as they interact with elders at home as well as with visitors at home and abroad. They can become as relaxed with that culture as with their own. In turn, we of the so-called developed world can learn from the traditions of Greenlanders who know the interactions of their place. Uummannaq is a 'take charge' community. As environmentalist and journalist Naomi Klein writes of 'place based' communities who know intimately the vagaries of 'their climate'.

*...[T] hat noticing small changes requires the kind of communion that comes from knowing a place deeply, not just as scenery but also as sustenance, and when local knowledge is passed on with a sense of sacred trust from one generation to the next (2014, 158-159).*

This book, which is based on the experience of 11 visits to Uummannaq from 2002 through 2016 and eight visits by Greenlanders to North America through 2015, is rich in material gathered through an array of shared experiences. Through the postings of Kunuunnguaq Fleischer, the patronage of Ann Andreasen, and the support of René Kristensen, friend and colleague with whom I have shared many adventures, Greenlanders generously and spontaneously opened their hearts and homes to me.

Modern agriculture in Itilleq, one of southern Greenland's deep fjords.

**Drummer**
*by Ronald (Qay) Apangalook.*
*Whalebone. Gambell,*
*St. Lawrence Island, Alaska.*
*2005. 33" x 14".*

# Cultural Geography

How did Western civilization become so estranged
from nonhuman nature, so oblivious to the presence of
other animals and the earth, that our current lifestyles and
activities contribute daily to the destruction of whole
ecosystems —whole forests, river valleys, oceans—and the
extinction of countless species.

*David Abram. The Spell of the Sensuous (1997, 137).*

Cultural geography—how water, topography, and latitude shape
culture—is a derivative of physical geography. Culture is the
set of human adaptations and mechanisms that enable a human
population to realize a condition of relative stability within a
given set of changed circumstances, particularly those associated with climate change and exogenous cultural intrusion.

The seven settlements established on the few scattered ice-free islands and
peninsulas of Uummannaq Fjord exemplify a hunting and gathering culture.
The people of these settlements have lived in harmony with the natural
world north of the Arctic Circle. Of necessity, the culture of the Uummannaq
Fjord continues to adapt to new circumstances in these northern latitudes.
The most important circumstances are climate change, and movement from
a subsistence economy to one that relies more and more on goods—bread

products, canned vegetables, Danish beer, toilet paper, diapers, dairy products, bottled water, sweets, clothing, kitchen appliances, hardware, occasional fresh fruits and vegetables, and strips of dog fur hanging in the produce department that women use for trim on the necks of women's traditional clothing—bought from the *Pilersuisoq* chain of government-sponsored retail outlets.

Historically, Greenland's indigenous peoples did not have fixed settlements in which to negotiate economic transactions. Rather, their culture was nomadic, and what was needed to sustain life was hunted—be it seal, whale, narwhal, walrus, reindeer (caribou), bird, fox, muskox, halibut, cod—while migrating from one location to another. Fixed human settlements in the geography of the Arctic were not present until European colonialism created a market for such goods as animal hides, fur, ivory, and fish. Popular images portray life in these high latitudes as an idyllic vision associated with the solitude of living above the Arctic Circle among the glaciers and icebergs.

clockwise from top left:

**This rock promontory is the iconic image of Ikerasak**
*This rock face reminds a viewer of Uummannaq.*
*This image looks from the waters of Ikerasak's port to its settlement.*
**Access to sea**
*In the 1920s, this landing in Ikerasak provided access to the sea and its resources. Image from Knudsen-Holm family archives, used with permission.*
**Early houses constructed of turf remain in today's Ikerasak.**

Through a composite of government economic policies that reduced
the value of support and services to its people, and significantly, that did not
compensate for the impact of climate change, some settlements have ceased
to exist. Because of greatly reduced population, other settlements barely
continue to exist. For example, the fjord settlements of Nuugaatsiaq and
Illorsuit, each with a current population of less than 100, are supported by an
array of government services—the *Pilersuisoq* stores, schools, postal services,
health care facilities, and heliports. (Unfortunately, the fate of Nuugaatsiaq

**Settlement of Ikerasak in late winter**
*This image of the village of Ikerasak encapsulates the solitude of winter with that of mortality.*

and Illorsuit was sealed in 2017, as outlined in paragraphs below, as these two communities were devastated by a landslide and subsequent tsunami.) As a generalization, the cost to provide goods and services to a fixed geographical community may be greater than the value of the extractive economy—hunting, fishing, and trapping—of the community. Meanwhile, the communities have become dependent on government services, and subsidies to communities from the government remain essential.

**Illorsuit**

*Left to right: Spring has arrived as evidenced by chained dogs, stacked sledges, and standing water.*

*Illorsuit was given the name 'unknown island' by the Dutch. The village of Ilulissat (meaning large houses), on the island of Illorsuit, is where American artist Rockwell Kent lived with his companion Salamina in the early 1930s. The village of Illulissat was erased in 2017 by a tsunami.*

In Uummannaq Fjord, settlements on islands and niches created by retreating glaciers are largely dependent on one commodity—halibut. Meanwhile, the demand for the goods and services required to sustain a modern European life style has expanded dramatically. The question with the growing imbalance between demand for goods and services, and the economic viability of the community has become whether or not government subsidies to these communities will continue. This same dilemma continues to face the fishery-based economies of the North Atlantic from Maine to Newfoundland and Labrador, which are variously dependent on finfish: halibut (turbot), diminutive sardine or capelin, the kingly salmon, the mighty cod; and/or shell fish, primarily lobster and shrimp.

The vulnerability of the Uummannaq settlements is not restricted to economic factors alone. On the evening of June 17, 2017, a substantial rock fall accompanied by glacial ice plunged about 1,000 meters into Karrat Fjord in the northerrn waters of Uummannaq Fjord, causing a tsunami. In a personal communication, René Kristensen reported that an unusually

large amount of ice in the fjord for that time of year helped reduce the size of waves generated by the rock fall, but the waves reaching shore were 10- to 15-meters in height. René went on to report:

> *In Nuugaatsiaq, destroyed were the settlement's power plant, factory, store, school, service house, and water tank. If the settlement's population ever returns, its infrastructure will need to be rebuilt, which will probably never happen. For Illorsuit, it is possible that people can return when the danger is over, which means when another slide at-risk has collapsed. When that happens, Illorsuit might suffer serious damage like Nuugaatsiaq did.*

Subsequent field research in July by Hermann Fritz (Georgia Institute of Technology) and others concluded that the vertical inertia of plunging debris generated a sharp upward water disturbance of up to 100 meters in height. These tall eruptions decreased in magnitude as the waves raced south across Uummannaq Fjord until arriving at the town of Uummannaq, as witnessed

**Freeze-dried laundry**

*With a lack of wood in the Arctic, particularly in the High Arctic, Greenlanders use whatever forms may drift ashore. Recycled sledge runners are often used as supports as are narwhal tusks. My eye is drawn to the delicacy of a clothesline or a drying rack, symbolic of the precarious balance in the Arctic of humans and all-encompassing, unrelenting nature. I am reminded of winter's laundry before the advent of the clothes dryer.*

*left to right:*
**Panorama of Nuugaatsiaq**
*With inuksuk in foreground, composition is from ridge overlooking the peninsula. Almost the entire settled landscape of Nuugaatsiaq is contained within this one narrow, short corridor reaching into the sea. The settlement of Nuugaatsiaq was erased in 2017 by a tsunami.*
**Traveling to Nuugaatsiaq by helicopter**
*Nuugaatsiaq is as far north as one can travel and still be in the Uummannaq Fjord. Helicopter is the only practical way to travel and view abstract ice formations. The flight engineer, a good friend Krister Jansson, lived up to his promise of an interesting flight.*

*top row:*

**School field trip**

*middle row:*

**The finely honed technology of a hunting culture**

*Boats, sledges, nets, harpoons, and floats serve this village that lies at the margin between two cultural worlds.*

*right:*

**Sealing, the traditional economic activity of Qaarsut**

*After a successful hunt, the community's skin shop processes and fashions sealskins into clothing and shoes. Qaarsut's skin shop, or 'factory', has since closed, a victim of intense media coverage of industrial hunting of baby harp seals in the very distant Gulf of St. Lawrence.*

**Settlement of Qaarsut**
*The road leads to Qaarsut. The ubiquitous Arctic Poppy (*Papaver radicatum*) is seen in the foreground while the signature profile of the mountains of Uummannaq is seen on the horizon.*

by René. There is a high probability of an additional rock slide for which Nuugaatsiaq and Illorsuit are in the danger zone, with only a few minutes warning time. It is too dangerous to live in these settlements and all inhabitants have been warned not to return for the indefinite future.

The collection of images that follows portrays the town of Uummannaq and the settlements arrayed around Uummannaq Fjord. They are Ikerasak, Illorsuit, Nuugaatsiaq, Qaarsut, Saattut, Uummannaq, and Ukkusigssat. *Uummannatsiaq*, the 'field school' of the Children's Home, where children learn and practice traditional skills, is located at the north end of Ikerasak Island. Uummannatsiaq is treated further in Chapter 4-Traditional Economy. Other images of these communities appear elsewhere in the book.

The images present a collage of the majesty of north Greenland with its white mountains and black crevasses—rock, sea, and ice; summer with its burning sun and brilliant blue sky; and winter with its twilight and darkness, when stars of the Milky Way convey the sharp contrasts of Arctic light. In this geography are the works of Inuit: settlements now with Scandinavian-type housing painted in a half-dozen primary colors; elaborate wooden walkways and stairs that cling vertically to Uummannaq's ascending ledges; dogs and sledges; drying racks, kayaks, and motor boats—and only an occasional snowmobile.

*from top:*
**Muktuk**
*René and Saattut resident and well-known hunter Jacob Løvstrom (Unartoq) feast on muktuk, the raw skin and blubber of the narwhal.*
**Saattut – rock outcrop**
*A small island with little elevation or ice, Saattut does not possess its own water supply, and water must be transported to the settlement.*
**Dog sledges stored for the season**
*Note the difference in sledge uprights. Sledge to left has upright fixed forward for hunting. Sledge to the right has upright fixed backward for fishing.*

### Ukkusissat

*This small fishing settlement lies in the northeastern reaches of Uummannaq Fjord. Ukkusissat is the settlement closest to Mármorilik and to the deactivated Black Angel Mine, which is high up on a cliff face, and can only be accessed by cable car. Historically, lead, zinc, and some silver have been extracted. There is occasional talk of reopening the mine.*

*clockwise from top left:*

**Walls of quarried granite**

*Massive walls provide a sense of timelessness to this place of worship. This image, of a recessed church window, was requested for the Greenland Prime Minister's office in Nuuk.*

**Uummannaq Harbor and petroleum product dependency**

*Like communities throughout the Arctic, energy in the form of fuel must be imported and stored to meet the needs for electricity, heating, and transportation.*

**Summer day**

*The church, constructed of quarried granite, has walls two feet thick.*

**Unlike the cover image, "Approaching Uummannaq by Helicopter", the island is not always awash in sunlight**

*As spring advances, fast ice along the shore breaks up into ice pans that hinder travel by both ice and water.*

**Sedna Totem**
*Ross Kayotak*
*Ivory with green stone base.*
*Iqaluit, Nunavut. 2001.*
*11" high with 2.5" base.*

**Drum Dance Totem**
*Ross Kayotak*
*Ivory with whalebone base.*
*Iqaluit, Nunavut. 2001*
*10" high with 5"*
*whalebone base.*

# 3

# Agents of Change: Leadership and Institutions of Uummannaq

The hunter-gatherer mind is humanity's most sophisticated combination of detailed knowledge and intuition. It is where direct experience and metaphor unite in a joint concern to know and use the truth.

*Hugh Brody. The Other Side of the World (2000, 292)*

Effective leadership in a community relies heavily on traditional social networks. In today's world, 'social network' includes traditional as well as such modern elements as *Facebook* and *Twitter*. In our modern techno-literate world, which encompasses Uummannaq as elsewhere, leaders benefit as much from the traditional social networks as from the ways in which social media enhance communications. While a culture of leadership in the Arctic has evolved over the generations, the final test lies in the perception by the community of the actions and decisions of its leadership. Uummannaq is fortunate to have several such leaders.

## Ann Andreasen

Ann, born in the Danish Faroe Islands, with a home in Denmark, and Director of Børnehjemmet, is a 'citizen of the Danish Realm', a political entity born of colonialism. Trained as a social worker, Ann knows how to work with many diverse cultures: she understands the individual personality and draws out the best from each person who interacts with her. In 2013, at the 250th anniversary of the founding of Uummannaq, in addition to many earlier awards, Ann was awarded the Silver Nersomaat Medal, Greenland's highest award, for her many years of 'extraordinary public service.' I had the good fortune to meet Ann while traveling through Uummannaq on my way to the settlement of Nuugaatsiaq.

**Ann Andreasen, Director of Uummannaq Children's Home**
*Ann makes a point in a discussion, one of many, in her home in Uummannaq.*

**René Kristensen**

*René is staff person for both the Children's Home (Børnehjemmet) and the Uummannaq Polar Institute. He is fluent in Danish and English, an excellent communicator, hunter and fisherman, skin diver and climber, and a leader. Here he helps his son Malik cross a glacial stream.*

## René Kristensen

René is a Dane who serves as educator, project manager, and assistant to Ann. He is a Social Educator and Project Leader for Børnehjemmet and Project Manager for the Uummannaq Polar Institute. He is also Director of the North Greenland Chapter of the International Appalachian Trail. René is a musician, strong hiker, passionate about the natural world, and a first-class friend. Like Ann, he possesses *simpatico* as appreciation for the individual.

## Børnehjemmet—The Children's Home

It was through Education Project Coordinator—and good friend— Kunuunnguaq Fleischer, then of the Greenland Ministry of Culture, Education, Research, and the Lutheran Church, that Ann Andreasen enters this narrative. Through a referral from Kunuunnguaq to Ann, I became a regular guest in Uummannaq and later a regular host, with my wife Lindsay, to Greenlanders who visited Maine.

Established in 1929 by the Danish colonial government of Greenland, there are currently two dozen children's homes, both public and private, in Greenland. Uummannaq's Children's Home, or *Børnehjemmet*, with an average enrollment of 35 residents, is one of Greenland's largest. It has evolved into both a residential and educational institution for young people from throughout Greenland who have been deemed by experts and the government "as in need from neglect, abuse, and abandonment". The goal of the Children's Home is to teach each child how to prevail over a harsh background but never to forget his/her Greenlandic origins. Through an emphasis on traditional skills, such as hunting and fishing, and through the experience of traveling, and living on the sea ice, the charges of the Children's Home become grounded in their Greenlandic heritage. In contrast to the colonial approach that 'nativeness' will dissipate with time, the Children's Home restores and reinforces traditional culture (for example, in *Selected Sources*, see Scranton, November 9, 2015). Further the Children's Home, in the insightful care of Ann Andreasen, links the traditional with the modern. In many respects, the Children's Home is analogous to an extended family.

The images that follow focus on the children of the Children's Home as well as other children in Uummannaq who live with their families and attend the public schools of the Uummannaq Fjord School District.

*clockwise from top left:*
**The Uummannaq Children's Home**
*Beyond Uummannaq's port and central commercial area, high up on one of the ridges that continue almost to the sheer rock walls of the monolith from which Uummannaq derives its name, is the Uummannaq Children's Home. The Government of Greenland sponsors all four public children's homes in Greenland.*
**Boy with flowers**
*July finds a toddler finding his way through a field of flowers.*
**Svend Hammeken**
*While on a visit to Qilakitsoq, young Svend found himself on a large rock with the tide coming in. He had to take some carefully coordinated leaps to get back to shore.*

The precept for the Children's Home, which guides all who are connected with the school, is: "As there are often unforeseen problems in life, it takes patience, observation and rational thought—not anger or violence—to resolve them." All the projects in which the residents of the Children's Home engage, from building houses of snow or wood to dog sledging, are experiences intended to form a Greenlandic identity and to develop social skills for both community living and for life away from home. As guests traveling in other cultures—on trips to Denmark and elsewhere in Europe, or to New York City, Boston, Washington DC, or Maine, these excursions provide a frame for cultural reference. In Denmark, young people from the Children's Home improve their language skills and absorb appropriate behaviors of another culture. Such behavior is then reinforced by emulation in the Children's Home.

*clockwise from top left:*

**Picnic on Ice**

*Now that the sun is shining after a long winter, let's have a picnic on the ice. The Children's Home works this way as both children and staff share in a spirit of spontaneity.*

**Young lady with sister**

*A fashionably dressed young lady holds her equally well-dressed sister.*

**Picnic Greenland style**

*No picnic is complete without seal, cooked or otherwise. An upturned sledge provides protection from wind.*

The charges of the Children's Home work on a set of skills from computer literacy to the crafting of traditional clothing from sealskins. Staff and visiting guests teach music and art along with retailing, painting, and electrical and mechanical skills. René has observed that around seventy-five percent of the graduates of the Children's Home go on to Denmark, or elsewhere, for further education, where they are exposed to other cultures. Most bring their skills back to Greenland, fulfilling the mission of the Children's Home.

Meanwhile, community elders provide instruction on the traditional ways of life. As part of the mission of the Children's Home, young Greenlanders are taken on a dog sledge expedition on the late winter ice of Uummannaq Fjord. Learning to drive a sledge and to care for the dogs, to fish and hunt, and to set up camp, helps these young Greenlanders, both boys and girls, pass from childhood to adulthood. Expeditions by the Children's Home are documented in a recent film—*Inuk*—produced by the Children's Home. *Inuk* tells the story of one Greenlandic youth who is tested in the harsh Arctic environment under the tutelage of an older hunter who is dealing with his own issues. Each grows from his friendship with the other.

**Victory**
*Though I am obviously from 'away', these two boys—assuming that I was lost—offered to help. I said 'no', that I was not lost. They both simultaneously flashed a 'V'.*

**Indian Face with Braids**
*by Clyde Drew*
*Woodland MicMac.*
*Moose antler.*
*St. Albans, Newfoundland.*
*3.5" base by 5.0" height.*

# 4

# Traditional Economy—
# *Siku*\*—Sea Ice Knowledge

All true wisdom is only to be found far from the
dwellings of man, in the great solitudes; and it can only
be obtained through suffering. Suffering and
privation are the only things that can open the mind
of man to that which is hidden from his fellows.
—Igjugarjuk of the Caribou Eskimos

Knud Rasmussen. *Across Arctic America: Narrative of the Fifth Thule Expedition*
*(1927 [1999], 381)*

During the Fifth Thule Expedition on Canada's Barren
Grounds among the Caribou Eskimos, Rasmussen
met Igjugarjuk, Chief of the Willow Folk, as the local angakoq,
a 'notable wizard' practiced in upholding local truths. Through
the seemingly supernatural, he upheld *Sila*, as a man's fate,
through 'a mixture of common sense, intelligence and wisdom' (Rasmussen
1927 [1999], 81). Commenting on the juxtaposition of the effectiveness
of spear and arrow versus the gun and ammunition, Rasmussen offers the
longer term summation that:

\* *Krupnik et al. 2010.*

*top to bottom:*
**Whale oil rendering**
*Heavy, massive iron cauldrons
are scattered throughout islands and
inlets of the North Atlantic and
Arctic, and will remain as time-
enduring artifacts of centuries of
European and American whaling.
These cauldrons are found near
the heliport in Uummannaq.*
**Model of whaling station in Red Bay,
Labrador**
*This scale model of a complete
whale oil rendering station would
be representative of European
oil rendering throughout the North
Atlantic. The brickwork that supports
the tripots also served a nautical
use, as ballast.*

> *"…The white man, through bringing certain perils in his train does
> nevertheless introduce a gentler code, and in many ways lightens the struggle
> for existence (Rasmussen 1927 [1999], 236)." …. "…the ingenious methods
> and implements of capture gave so rich a yield as to cover also the dead
> seasons where no game was to be had…(Rasmussen 1927 [1999], 73)."
> Although "The gun has immediate advantages, but it is doubtful whether it
> pays better in the long run…. it should be borne in mind that arrow and
> spear did their work silently….Now, since the introduction of firearms…
> famine has frequently resulted (Rasmussen 1927 [1999], 75)."*

The essential question raised by Rasmussen is whether the ways of a traditional subsistence economy, and later within this text, whether an indigenous
economy that bypasses both the agricultural and industrial revolutions,
can co-exist within the context of today's global exchange market economy?
As well, is there value to be learned by the world from Arctic subsistence
economies as we face an increasing complexity of consumptive ways and

**Shore-fast ice and iceberg ice**
*In this early spring, our boat is positioned between two forms of ice. In background is an iceberg calved from one of Greenland's glaciers. In foreground is shore-fast ice, an annual winter ice linked to shore, now in a state of decomposition.*

climate change on the home we all share, Planet Earth; and to what extent can a worldwide consumptive market economy take from the resources of nature, which includes *homo sapiens*?

Harvesting life from Arctic seas, local and global, is almost epochal in duration. Following the Norse, the next global connection came to Uummannaq in the form of Dutch whalers in the 17th century, followed by Scots, English, and New England whalers. Tripots—cast iron cauldrons used to render oil from blubber are found throughout the North Atlantic. Once whale populations plummeted, however, tripot installations were abandoned. Abandoned tripots, mementos of an industry long gone, are found throughout the Maritime Far Northeast (Fitzhugh and Richard 2014), including the area around Uummannaq. While exploring the Lower North Shore along the Gulf of St. Lawrence, we often came across an iron tripot—perhaps Basque, English, Danish, American—standing the test of time, on the smallest dot of an island. The Basques and the Dutch were particularly active throughout North Atlantic and Arctic waters as shown above in the image of a Dutch whale oil rendering station in Red Bay, Labrador. However successful Basque whalers were, they did not use tripots. Rather they set a number of big pots filled with blubber on stone hearths (Fitzhugh, personal communication, January 2016). European whaling introduced west Greenlanders to the European economy and manufactured goods that did not greatly alter local subsistence practices, which had been in place for thousands of years. During my visits to Uummannaq I have experienced both subsistence and market economies, and the resource extraction activities of both.

## Hunting

During my travels to this part of Greenland, which started more than
a decade ago, there has often been a condition of either no ice or ice that is
unsafe for hunting, usually of seals. When ice is present in Uummannaq
Fjord, it is usually on the northern fringe of the fjord in the waters around
Nuugaatsiaq. Because I wanted to learn more about conditions for hunting,
Kunuunnguaq Fleischer arranged a visit to the northernmost settlement
of Nuugaatsiaq to view—and participate in—more traditional hunting
practices. On my first day, Ole Møller, a local hunter and fisherman, took me
seal hunting on the ice, which we reached by speedboat. Attempting to walk
towards our prey, we found the ice unsafe. Later we located a floe, although
slushy on the surface, which was solid enough to support our weight. Using a
*toorut*, a long metal-tipped wooden pole (typically 2m to 3m in length) to test
the ice, Ole navigated our way. At a distance of about 75 meters, he began
to crawl towards a ringed seal (*Pusa hispida*) behind a white camouflage blind
(*qamutaasaq* or *taalutaq*) made of a small square of canvas, through which
the barrel of his rifle protruded.

**Ringed seal (Pusa hispida) shot on ice**
*On another more secure ice pan, Ole Møller inches forward—
methodically testing the ice with his toorut, the metal-tipped
wooden pole. A ringed seal rests at a distance of about 150m
(500ft). It is time to drop to the prone position. Out of sight and
with neither sound nor smell, Ole advances slowly forward
with his rifle barrel protruding through a patch of white canvas
acting as camouflage. Soon, with one shot, there is a kill. With
a line through a slit in the seal's throat and then out the mouth,
Ole drags the seal back to the boat and home for fresh meat.*

*left to right:*

**Travel with Unartoq**

*Unartoq's sledge is festooned with all kinds of gear, ready for any contingency, be it forced bivouac on the ice, breakthrough of ice, hunting, fishing, or trapping.*

**Ole Jørgen Hammeken with his large dog team**

*Here dogs fan out as opposed to Alaska where dog teams travel in a file. On ice, the 'fan' configuration provides a margin of safety; in case a dog breaks through the ice, other dogs are not pulled down into frigid Arctic water. A simple 'line' configuration is good for sledging through densely forested landscapes, but not over ice-bound conditions over a wide expanse of water.*

In the days that followed we spent most of our time fishing from his trawler Helena for halibut (*Reinhardtius hippoglossoides*) by long line and net. We also caught salt-water catfish (*Anarhichas lupus*) and the huge Greenland shark (*Somniosus microcephalus*). The latter serves only as dog food. Acquiring dog food from the sea saves money and time, a lot of both. On hunting trips, many dog team drivers use bagged commercial dry dog food, specially blended for Arctic dog teams, but this is very expensive. Other than price, the primary difference between using dried dog food versus fresh fish and game is that the dry food requires less space on the sledge.

On a second seal-hunting trip, in 2012, I traveled with 'Unartoq' (Jakob Løvstrom) and his dog team. He and I were the oldest men on the hunt—and I am older than he. I was fortunate to travel with Unartoq ('kind face'), as he is a respected hunter. Although I speak no Greenlandic and he no English, we effectively communicate through facial expressions and hand signs. Ole Jørgen Hammeken, too, was on the hunt with a team of 15 dogs.

In early evening, we found a bivouac site on the ice that was devoid of cracks and other irregularities. There was no wind, but the red sky suggested that the next day would be pleasant as per an old sailor's saw that goes: *red skies at night, sailors delight, red skies in the morning, sailors take warning*. A red, low-angle sun cast shadows across the drifts. For the night, the dogs were secured by digging down into the ice with the toorut, making two vertical insertions and then connecting them under the ice with a horizontal channel. A line is then fixed to this construction as an anchor point. We assembled the sledges into pairs with each sledge being placed lengthwise against another to form a two-sledge platform with a width of about 2m (6ft) and a length of better than 2.6m (8ft). A canvas tarp was then strung over the sledges to produce a tent that accommodated all five of us. Although the month was May, it was more like January in Maine. Before we bedded down for the night, Unartoq and I enjoyed the evening. It was a cold night.

## Readying dog tie-downs

*No one travels on the ice without a toorut. Digging down and then tunneling a horizontal wrap-around in the ice to another parallel hole and then up-and-out enables driver to secure dogs without hammering a steel rod or other tethering device into intensely cold, hard ice. This is a quick and easy method of tether placement. When breaking camp, there are no fixtures to be removed from the ice with frozen hands and there is nothing left behind at spring melt to be ingested by a fish or seal.*

*clockwise from top left:*

## Rest break

*Dogs and drivers take a break: drivers check out dogs and the sledges; dogs eat snow to replenish their water reserves and rest from the exhaustion of running and pulling a sledge with at least one rider.*

## Evening's bivouac

*With Unartoq, we rest on a sledge, absorbing the last rays of light of setting sun. With varying degrees of snugness, sledges are outfitted with a canvas tarp to create sleeping quarters. The dogs burrow into the snow and wait for morning.*

**Hunter and hunted**
*The usual objective of harvesting a seal has been modified to capture an image of a obliging seal.*

The grand total of seals harvested by some eighteen hunters, a dozen sledges, and dozens of dogs, was one ringed seal. That seal was not shot; rather Unartoq caught it with a net. Unfortunately, net-caught seals are not as tasty as are seals that have been shot. Suffocation deprives the blood supply of oxygen, which in turn degrades the flavor of the meat. In an early ice out event in April 2016, we traveled by boat to find ice on which to dog sledge. A curious ringed seal swam along with us.

Do not confuse these traditional subsistence hunts for ringed seal with the industrial-scale seal hunting for 'white coats' in the Gulf of St. Lawrence, Magdalene Islands, and off the North Atlantic waters of Newfoundland. For the latter, only the hide of the newborn harp seal (*Pusa groenlandicus*) is used. In Greenland, the non-migratory ringed seal is the preferred prey, because of flavor, and the hunting party may be only one, two, or just a few hunters. These indigenous hunts are characterized as 'subsistence' hunts. They are not large-scale kills just for seal pelts but for whole animals. The meat becomes part of the diet, and skins are made into clothing or boots for the Children's Home. Elsewhere in Uummannaq, fat may be rendered to make broth for soup. Sealskin may also be used to sheathe boats or tents as well as feed dogs.

**Wildlife is abundant and well traveled**
*The well-traveled Greenland seal (*Phoca groenlandica*) on an iceberg, travels from the waters of Greenland to the ice-laden waters of Newfoundland and into the Gulf of St. Lawrence during which time mother seal whelps a pup known as a 'whitecoat'. Both mother and offspring then journey apart to Greenland.*

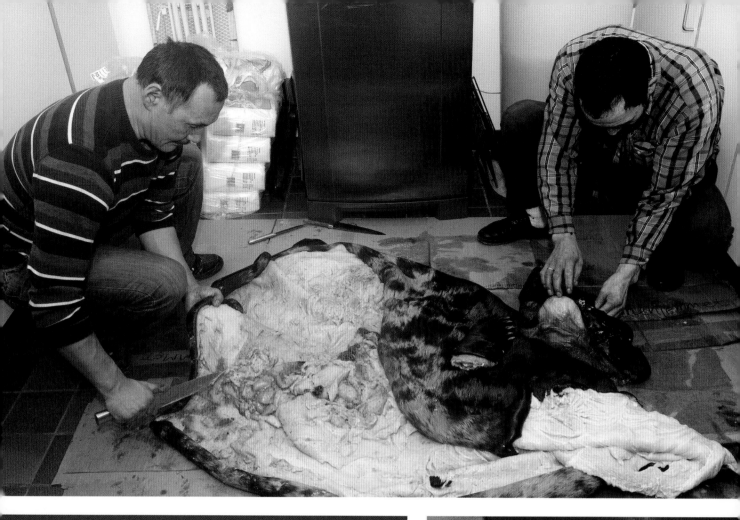

*top to bottom:*

**Food and clothing**

*Two hunters who are employed by the Children's Home skin and butcher a freshly killed seal, which will be used for clothing, boots, and food.*

**Sustainable hunt labeling**

*To utilize a 'best practices' approach to marketing seal products, a label is affixed to each sealskin, to inform the potential buyer that the seal was taken by traditional subsistence practices. The success of such ventures has not saved subsistence seal hunting, though, as indicated by closure of the local skin factory in Qaarsut.*

In Uummannaq, seals are usually used for boots, clothing, and food for the Children's Home. Rarely now, with the bans on seal products in the United States and Europe, do seal products, even those harvested through Inuit practices of sustainable sealing, go to commercial markets. My sense is that uncertainty in global markets, and sea mammal product restrictions imposed by the European Union (EU) and other jurisdictions, have had a huge impact on Greenland exports in recent years.

Although fewer Greenlanders engage in hunting, and while fewer seals are being taken and sold, the hunter remains the central emblematic symbol of traditional Greenlandic culture. He represents the respected leader in family and settlement structure. Fishing does not fulfill these cultural needs. Although now there is much more fishing than hunting, it is valued simply as an economic activity. Although the import ban on Canada's northwest Atlantic harp seal continues, systems are now in place to certify for market sea mammal products generated by 'Aboriginal' communities.

Ray Weaver writes that even though much of Greenland is "becoming urbanized, it is still a lifestyle very much based in nature." He quotes Denmark's *Jylland's-Posten* newspaper:

> *It is still a lifestyle based on finding food just outside one's door and the World Wildlife Fund (WWF) prefers that Greenlanders trap seals rather than import chicken and increase the world's carbon footprint.*

It was not the Inuit who participated in the massive clubbing of baby harp seals, yet the unintended consequences of international bans have hurt them badly. The WWF has finally acknowledged the harm to subsistence hunters caused by its dragnet (2013), and Greenpeace, which spearheaded the anti-seal hunt campaign following a Canadian cull, is belatedly coming to the Greenlanders' aid. The organization is blamed by Canadian Inuit for plunging their communities into poverty since the 1960s. (May 16, 2015).

The European Commission now authorizes trade in seal products:

> *The seal hunt is part of the economy, culture and identity of the Inuit and other indigenous communities and it contributes greatly to their subsistence and development. For this reason, the Regulation provides for an Inuit exception. It allows the placing on the (European) Union market of seal products, which result from hunts traditionally conducted by Inuit and other indigenous communities. (European Commission: Environment. October 26, 2015)*

As I understand, travelers returning to Europe from the Arctic who enter a Common Market nation may now import seal products either worn on their person or contained in their luggage for personal use and for family members.

## Fishing

In Greenland, fishing is a serious business, supplanting hunting in the cash economy. As soon as ice conditions permit, boats set out for the deep waters of Uummannaq Fjord.

While near the Store Glacier (Map 3), René and I, and the rest of the crew, stopped to fish for capelin (*Mallotus villosus*). Instead of fishing poles, we used large gaff hooks bound to the end of a pole. A fisherman plunges the pole and hook into the water and then quickly yanks it up. The surface area on the topside of the hook is large enough to provide a relatively flat platform on which to catch small fish through the momentum of the jigging motion. I pulled up four fish in one plunge, for which Unartoq gave me a 'thumbs up' and a 'ten' sign. We gathered mussels at the northern end of

Ikerasak. Returning to Uummannatsiaq, our camp at the north end of
Ikerasak Island, there was another boat, this one loaded with capelin. Later,
Children's Home staff member Rebekka Jørgensen made our tasty dinner by
pan-frying the fish.

The following day, Ann called to invite me to go long-line fishing with Karl
Fleischer, a townsman. Long-line fishing began in Greenland only in the
1960s. Until then, fishing was considered woman's work, and was done with a
pole and line. In those days, men were culturally identified through their
iconic role as hunters.

**Fishing—a year-round activity**
*Whether operating with long lines from a dog sledge platform or from a boat, fishing —particularly for halibut—has become a year-round economic mainstay of the cash economy.*

Long-line fishing is done through a rectangular hole in the ice. It is not easy to cut the hole and keep it open. A frame is installed over the hole, on which a roll of orange poly line with a two-sided hand crank is positioned. In this case, the roll has 800m (2,600ft) of line and 180 m of black leader for an effective long line length of 980m (3,215ft), almost 1 km (.6 mi), to which more than 350 green sidelines are attached, each with a hook. Each hook is baited with a bit of octopus. A rectangular piece of plywood with a rock for weight is attached to the far end of the line. Warped plywood is located between the screen of long lines with hooks and sledge. This device must drift with the current while being heavy enough to sink: if it does not sink it will not catch deep-swimming halibut.

**Carl Fleischer and Will at fishing station**
*Ready with a long line played out the previous day, Carl and I prepare to reel in the catch. Although it is spring, solid ice has closed the fish hole. With his toorut, Carl re-opens the hole to bring in the catch. Hopefully it is halibut* (Reinhardtius hippoglossoides)*, also known as Greenland halibut.*

As we worked, we reeled in a long-line loaded with Greenland halibut (*Reinharditus hippoglossoides*), the primary cash fish, and sculpin (*Myoxocephalus scorpius*) known locally as *tupissut*, a locally prized good eating fish. We also landed catfish (some for export), skate, and grenadier, the latter two tossed aside as trash fish. Greenland's primary finfish export is halibut. Over the many decades of the halibut fishery, the average size of a halibut fish has

*clockwise from top left:*

**Halibut and by-catch**
*Many halibut are caught for export, with a sizeable by-catch of fish such as sculpin, red fish, skate, and shark: some of the latter will be used to feed sledge dogs. Here, Carl is removing a good-sized halibut from a hook.*

**The catch in the 1920s**
*Compare the previous image with one almost a century old from the Knudsen-Holm collection: there is certainly a significant size difference. Today's higher fish catch rate reflects a younger fish population of smaller size. Image from Knudsen-Holm family archives used with permission.*

**Excellent food fish**
*Ole Møller displays a Redfish that he caught in his net set the previous day. Of the Sabastinae family, there are three species of Redfish. This particular catch is either the larger Sebastes marinus or the deepwater Sebastes mentella. This fish will yield two good-sized, white slabs of meat. (Gensbol 2004, 146-147).*

decreased. Also caught is the *Sebates* (Redfish), a scaly, rotund, big-eyed fish. Its flesh is cod-like, but the fish is difficult to de-scale, skin, and filet. Many of these species are deep-water fish ranging to depths of 1,200m (3,900ft).

By May it had been six or seven months since the *Pilersuisoq* (the general store) was able to replenish its stocks of fruit, vegetables, and other food-stuffs. When I heard that a Royal Arctic ship was approaching, I walked from the village to the harbor entrance to take photos. I had no toorut or any other rod with which to check the firmness of the ice, but I saw four people de-scend onto the ice from the end of the pier, so I continued in that direction. Soon, a Royal Arctic Line ship, the *Mary Arctica* appeared with its deck three to six deep in stacked, empty cargo containers—save one loaded with fresh fruit and vegetables for the town.

Freezer lockers in Uummannaq and other fishing settlements throughout the fjord were full of processed fish, and this cargo ship was here to load the halibut that had been caught throughout the Uummannaq Fjord region.

Removal of stored fish would allow the fishery to re-open. As the ship worked back-and-forth to establish an open channel in the water, hunters hurried to release lashings from the ice to which dogs were tied. The rocking motion of the ship continued for a good two hours in a cold wind blowing off the ice. Once the *Mary Arctica* docked next to the fish plant, cranes transferred tons of frozen halibut onto the ship. Meanwhile, snow machines from outlying settlements began to arrive dragging sledges loaded with halibut bound for Europe and Asia.

From fjord settlements, such as Nuugaatsiaq and Ikerasak, most of the halibut and some catfish first go to the local Royal Greenland plant for processing and then to Uummannaq for export. While it is illegal to hunt or fish from snow machines, it is legal to transport fish that have been processed. Most catfish, along with dried shark meat, remains in the community for dog food. Shark must be stored on high racks so the dogs cannot reach it. Fresh shark is poisonous to the dogs because of the high concentration of ammonia in its flesh. During drying, the ammonia is neutralized and the meat becomes safe for the dogs.

**The Mary Arctica slowly and laboriously breaks a channel into port**
*As ice shatters, sea gulls converge to take advantage of open water and of fish that are churned up by the ship's propellers.*

*top to bottom:*
**Fish inventories delivered by snow machine converge on Uummannaq**
*Drivers may use snow machines throughout the settlements of Uummannaq Fjord; here they are used to bring the stored catch of halibut to Uummannaq for shipment, primarily to Europe and Asia.*
**Back to Nuugaatsiaq**
*On racks high enough to be out of reach of ravenous dogs, shark meat is dried, until no longer toxic, for dog food.*

With René and a party of boys from the Children's Home, we again meet Jorgen Dahl at the Children's Home annex in Ikerasak, where he is the caretaker. Jorgen described how the local Inuit hunting and gathering practices evolved over the previous 900 years (Map 3). Every spring there is a broad lead or a crack in the ice that develops off the southern tip of Nuussuaq Peninsula. Here, Greenlanders once came to fish. There were special places for gathering bird's eggs and for collecting mussels at the northern tip of Ikerasak Island. From Parnat on Storøen Island, berries were harvested to eat and for coloring animal skins. Located further to the east on Storøen Island, red dye was made from iron-bearing sand. Agpart Island, due north of

**Gathering fossil fuel in Greenland**
*Inger Knudsen gathers herbaceous plant runners, which are abundant on the surface of Arctic tundra. With little year-round sunlight and poor biotic soil, these plants, usually members of the willow family, are the few forms of wood-like organic fuel produced by photosynthesis available in the Arctic. Image from Knudsen-Holm family archives used with permission.*

Uummannaq island, was a source for bird skins, with women in an umiak doing the collecting. Jorgen tells us that Inuit could not recount travel in our 'clock' time. Rather, they would tell travel distance in terms of eating treats, drinking coffee and smoking a pipe. This would be gauged in increments of European goods such as '2 tobacco', '3 tobacco', '1 coffee', and '4 coffee', that is, the time traveled before stopping to have one coffee or other treat. To this day—perhaps a holdover—the driver of a boat will stop in mid route, often surrounded by icebergs, for a coffee.

Despite increasing connections with the outside world, Uummannaq remains a remote hunter/fisher or 'gatherer' culture. 'Gathering' is mostly from the sea. Changes, however, have occurred. What we term an 'economy' has seen Uummannaq move away from local subsistence to that of an export market economy. Dependency on the halibut fishery—along with the shrimp fishery is but a minor player in Uummannaq's economy. But, it is an indicator of increasing interdependency, as is tourism, with the outside world.

Friend René Kristensen recently commented: halibut fishing from a dog sledge is being rapidly replaced by fishing from a tracked, gasoline powered snow machine. Dogs do not need to be fed and maintained nor does the fisherman need to remain out on the ice for days. Rather, halibut fishing is increasingly a daily trip by snow machine out on the ice. Stocks of halibut appear to be plentiful and prices are good, and a nice income is ensured for the fisherman.

The transition from dog team to snow machine, and perhaps powerboat, is accompanied by the increasing integration of subsistence fishing into the market economy. Meanwhile, movement away from a kinship structure in which a successful hunter shares his catch with the elderly is more than economic; it is cultural, with a likely change in social structure. There is no going back.

Film producer Mike Magidson, formerly of California, has produced two insightful films on Greenland which focus on Uummannaq, the first being *Inuk*. In his second film, *Call of the Ice*, he was the only actor. Upon receiving thorough training from renowned hunter Unartoq in hunting, fishing, and driving dogs, he traveled alone out on the ice where he tried his hand at traditional subsistence living. After two weeks of futile efforts at both hunting and fishing and without success at either, Mike sledged back to Uummannaq. Upon his return, Mike asked how long it would take to become a hunter. The answer: "seven generations". We outsiders do not give the complexities and time-tested effectiveness of Arctic culture its just due.

**Man with Baby**
*by Napachie Ashoona.*
*Greenish black soapstone.*
*Cape Dorset, Baffin,*
*Nunavut.*
*7" high x 3" wide.*

# 5

# Current Economy— The Development of Tourism

There will come a time... when the goal that was the Arctic wilderness will have been explored, and there will be nothing left to find. But our longing for a simple life will be unsatisfied; we will continue to search for silent places.

*Joanna Kavenna. The Ice Museum: In Search of the Lost Land of Thule (2005, 39)*

The geography and culture of Uummannaq, as explored in Chapters 2 and 8, holds an innate attraction for the curious and adventurous traveler—particularly so in the 21st century when accelerated glacial movement, increased calving of icebergs, and a shrinking ice cap—consequences of climate change—have become of such concern. A goal of culture is to convey the cumulative knowledge of that culture from one generation to the next. For an Arctic hunting culture, that means applying its ancient record of effectively knowing how to work with environmental conditions of wind, snow, low temperature, and in particular ice conditions. Yet, changing environmental conditions require modifications to the culture.

As reported by the media, the change in Arctic climate has raised a demand for a new economic activity in the Arctic regions of Canada and Greenland—adventure travel and tourism. Many people outside the Arctic now have the luxury of money, time, and desire for travel. The threatened ecosystem of the Arctic has become attractive to tourists much like

**Kangerlussuaq**
*Located at the far inland end of Søndre Strømfjord in the south of Greenland, and an hour by air from Ilulissat, Kangerlussuaq is the aerial hub in Greenland for international travel.*

the threatened ecosystems of Patagonia in Argentina and Chile, the Galapagos Islands of Ecuador, Antarctica, and South Georgia. Modern technology has created a dilemma: industrial technology is a major contributor to global degradation, and with relatively inexpensive air travel more of us want and are able to view, first hand, what technology has done to the planet's ice caps. So, we hop on a large jet, which expels heat-trapping gases, to see what we have done to the ecosystem. The increased calving of icebergs caused largely by human-created global warming becomes the impetus for a new economic activity in the Arctic—seemingly benign travel and tourism. Apparently our species is attracted by the splendor of disaster. Are we creatures of the Anthropocene, faced with an intractable problem, with a Gordian knot? Or, might visitors to these threatened places become proselytizers for a less consumptive humanity?

For tourism to expand in the Uummannaq Fjord region does not require an expansion of support amenities such as hotels, restaurants, and local transportation. Such amenities already exist on the south side of the Nuussuaq Peninsula in Ilulissat. While travel in Uummannaq Fjord is an adventure unsurpassed elsewhere in the Arctic, Greenland remains a land with few tourists, in part because transportation to Greenland as well as within Greenland is limited to water and air. Both are expensive.

**Travel by helicopter to Uummannaq**
*Throughout most of Greenland, the helicopter is the most practical mode of transportation. Image is from a photo opportunity for both '60 Minutes' crew and those of us on the ground. Given an unforgiving landscape of mountains and glaciers, forget improvised landings.*

## Getting there

Transport by air to Greenland is not for the faint-hearted. Air Greenland helicopter pilot Stefan Rahmberg recounts a pilot saying: "I would rather be on the ground wishing that I was in the air, than in the air wishing that I was on the ground." The case in point, realized by this bit of wisdom, is the visibility on the Nuussuaq Peninsula which we fly over from Ilulissat on its south side to Qaarsut on the north side. Visibility of at least 900ft vertical and 1500m horizontal is required to fly. On one occasion, visibility at Ilulissat airport was 300ft. Visibility at Qaarsut was 100ft vertical and 600m horizontal. Aeronautical protocol expresses distance above the earth's surface in feet but horizontal distance in meters. In this case, Pilot Rahmberg chose to remain on the ground.

Whiteouts that cut off forward visibility or visibility up or down, are common. During World War II, with literally no fixed point of reference, many military pilots, even flying above 3,000m (10,000ft), became totally disoriented by horizon-to-horizon whiteness, a condition further aggravated by cloud cover; and sometimes crashed into the Greenland Ice Sheet at elevations up to 3,000m. Given the severity of northern weather, the great distances involved, and the mountainous terrain, emergency landings are fraught with potentially

**Helicopter pilots often become long-time friends**
*Given the close proximity of pilots and passengers, and through frequent travel, close relationships can form.*

fatal danger. Bear in mind that only the perimeter of Greenland is—in places—ice free. Even in those narrow land margins, the terrain is not flat but may be fragmented by bedrock, moraines, and boulders deposited by glaciers. Air travel in the Arctic is guided by a more stringent set of conditions and rules than that of flights in temperate, populated regions with less challenging topography. The message for the traveler is patience, which is markedly better than the alternatives.

For visitors to Uummannaq or Ilulissat who travel by air, the international carrier will be either Air Greenland or Air Iceland. If it is Air Greenland, the

**To Greenland by sea**
*Whether piloting one's own sailboat or as passenger on windjammer or modern tourist vessel, travel by sea from Europe to Greenland is becoming increasingly common. In part, increased travel by sea is a function of milder weather that permits a longer sailing season and more frequent sailings.*

flight will land at Kangerlussuaq, which is the hub of Air Greenland. The next flight link to a Greenlandic destination will be a propeller driven aircraft to Ilulissat or Qaarsut. For the hop from the Nuussuaq Peninsula to Uummannaq, the flight is by an Air Greenland helicopter. This is only a 10-or-so minute flight to the heliport on Uummannaq—if weather permits. But, if not, Air Greenland pilots are gregarious people: maybe it will be a meal or tales of flying exploits. Stories result in the formation of many friendships spanning the North Atlantic.

A few travelers will arrive by water, traveling in their own craft, such as the *Killary Flyer* from Ireland with its crew of kayakers. Most, though, arrive in tour ships from Europe, or from Canada via Adventure Canada cruises.

## Visiting Ilulissat or Uummannaq

# Ilulissat

The weather in Ilulissat (formerly Jakobshavn), is influenced by latitude, the North Atlantic Drift (a warm water current associated with the Gulf Stream), and by the tremendous volume of ice discharged into Disko Bay. A May snowstorm is not the least bit unusual, appearing to render the airstrip a little problematic.

**Ilulissat airport**
*Just to the north of town, with icebergs only a few meters from the airstrip, fixed-wing aircraft fly into Ilulissat to link Uummannaq with Kangerlussuaq and Nuuk.*

Many visitors to this part of Greenland select Ilulissat as a final destination, to view the Jakobshavn Isbrae (Glacier), which is the largest ice floe emanating from the Greenland Ice Sheet (see Chapter 7-Climate Change). Whether entering or leaving Ilulissat, with the right weather conditions the traveler is treated to grand views of Jakobshavn Isbrae. Ilulissat is a point-of-transit for

**Aerial view of the Arctic Hotel and its aluminum igloos**
*The Arctic Hotel is located north of town on a peninsula that presents a commanding view of both the town of Ilulissat and its nearby icebergs. Depending on the weather, navigating in or out of the port can challenge any pilot.*

visitors to Uummannaq. Ilulissat is definitely upscale, a choice place to visit—particularly to view its city-size icebergs calving into Disko Bay. Overwhelming the sights around Ilulissat is the ice that dominates both land and seascape. While flying above Ilulissat, a visitor spots the four-star Arctic Hotel, prominently sited on a hill just outside of town. This elevation affords

*clockwise from top:*
**Icebergs measured in kilotons, like this one, calved from the Jakobshavn Glacier**
*This one iceberg is larger than the town of Ilulissat, which can be seen in the distance.*
**Jakobshavn icebergs from Arctic Hotel**
*Navigation, just getting in or out of port, can be problematic.*
**Port of Ilulissat**
*Fishing, tourism, and maritime maintenance provide a solid economic base for Ilulissat.*
**View of Ilulissat from the Arctic Hotel**
*On an early spring morning with full light and still air, the north side of the entrance to Ilulissat's port is fully illuminated by a pristine atmosphere found only in the Arctic.*

*clockwise from top:*

**Knud Rasmussen remembered**

*In the 1930s, Danish royalty and colonial officials assist in the dedication of a stone monument to the memory of Knud Rasmussen (godfather to Inger Knudsen) who passed in 1933 at the age of 54. Aage Knudsen, Denmark's northern District Manager, with formal top hat in hand, presides over the dedication. To right of monument is Else with their twin sons Per and Ib. Images from Knudsen-Holm family archives used with permission.*

**Knud Rasmussen's Home in Ilulissat**

*The Rasmussen homestead has been well maintained. Note in the foreground a traditional turf-reinforced Greenlandic home.*

an excellent view of both the town and the icebergs. A halibut or muskox burger with a local brew in the Hotel's 'Ferdinand Bar & Grill' may be enjoyed while enjoying the view of the bay, and a choice selection of Greenland arts and crafts may be found in the town. Today, Ilulissat is an air hub; historically, it has served as a major embarkation port for points north since the time of Dutch whalers in the 17th century.

Historical images from the Knudsen-Holm collection portray the dedication in the 1930s of a monument to the cultural hero Knud Rasmussen, 'father of Greenland'. In the larger image is Aage Knudsen (with top hat), *Kolonibestyrer* of North Greenland District. The monument is dedicated to the memory of Knud Rasmussen, 'Father of Eskimology', anthropologist, ethnographer, and polar explorer by dog sledge, from Greenland to Alaska. The home of Knud Rasmussen continues to be meticulously maintained.

**Visitors from Japan**

*With dinner and entertainment arranged by Ann Andreasen, Japanese visitors walk up hill to the town's high school where they enjoy a music concert. Ann, in black and white jacket, speaks through a tour guide to a gentleman who has been honored internationally for his then recent climb of Mt. Everest.*

## Uummannaq

While visitors to Uummannaq experience fewer helicopter tours, craft outlets, and lodging options than visitors to Ilulissat, there is more exposure for the visitor to a relatively undisturbed place and its people. As with any new experience, a visitor needs to be curious enough to explore and ask questions. The Arctic is neither an American Disney World nor a Danish Tivoli Gardens. While there are no large restaurants along the main street, right across from the harbor is the chic Emmacafé, operated by Winnie Johnson. Or, in conjunction with a tour operator, Ann Andreasen can arrange for a tour,

*this page, from top:*
**Visitors from Europe**
*A group of Swiss and Russian tourists come ashore with their guides to a hosted dinner at Uummannaq's high school.*
**Emmacafé**
*The proprietress of this waterfront cafe, Winnie Johnson, supplies delicious French fries, beer and coffee. On sunny days, patrons bask in the warmth while watching tourists disembark from landing craft docked on the other side of the street.*

as she did for a group of Swiss and Russian visitors, or, just as likely,
a Children's Home dinner or a concert at the Uummannaq High School,
as for a group of Japanese visitors.

## Two halves of a working whole

From a transportation perspective, Ilulissat, located on the mainland,
is better suited for tourism than Uummannaq, which is an island. Ilulissat
receives fixed wing aircraft from both Air Greenland and Air Iceland.
The only practical way to reach Uummannaq by air is by helicopter.

Consequently, most tourism infrastructure, such as hotels, restaurants, outfitters, tour operators, and gift shops are located on the south side of the Nuussuaq Peninsula in Ilulissat. Within the context of tourism, remoteness attracts. The edge that the traveler to Uummannaq enjoys is cultural tourism in traditional settlements that are accessible only by boat. There are no roads between settlements—only within a settlement—and then they are more akin to paths arrayed on wooden scaffolding. The exception is by auto or truck or taxi (credit cards accepted) on winter's ice, whenever there is ice. It is here in Uummannaq that recreational, cultural, and environmental tourism are readily available in the form of kayaking, backpacking, and dog sledging, or by accompanying hunters and fishermen as they seek prey on land or sea.

In essence, Uummannaq and Ilulissat offer a choice of experiences. The two towns complement each other, each offering a different kind of experience. Ilulissat offers flights over and onto the Jakobshavn Isbrae (Glacier), luxury lodging, fine dining, and first class shopping. Uummannaq offers the traveler an adventure by dog sledge or small boat operated by local fishermen and hunters. Meals can be arranged through the Children's Home, the Emmacafé, or through fishermen and hunters. With peninsulas, icebergs, and archaeological sites, and seven settlements outside the island municipality of Uummannaq, emersion in a broad and varied Greenland culture is readily available.

With Arctic ice melt and changing climate, the volume of northern travelers has increased dramatically—not only by plane but also by ship. My first visit to Greenland in 2002 was by ship, a Russian vessel contracted by Adventure Canada. Over the years, I have seen an increase in cruise ships to Uummannaq. British tourists, for instance, may now arrive on a Norwegian cruise ship. At least two Scandinavian cruise liners visit Uummannaq weekly during the summer months. There is enough tourist activity to have a commercial impact. A definite advantage of traveling by cruise ships to Uummannaq is that the visitor brings along his/her own bed and board.

Greenland may never become a mass tourist destination for two reasons: the cost in time, money, and effort required to put an adventure together, and the shortage of amenities to support tourism. Everything must be imported. For Greenland to become a mass tourist destination would para- doxically compromise what visitors are coming to experience: Arctic nature, exotic culture, adventure, recreation, and to witness the dynamics of climate change. Greenlandic arts and crafts—like their Canadian Arctic counterparts—have become highly prized and are quite collectable. However, Greenlandic handicrafts created by native artists from Arctic sea mammals cannot be imported into the United States. Products made from caribou (reindeer) or muskox are permissible as are carvings made from stone or mineral. Clothing made from reindeer as well as intricate glass beadwork may be purchased.

**Pierre Auzias**
*Pierre has a studio in central Uummannaq, high on a ledge overlooking the harbor, where he teaches visual arts and sells the work of local artists as well as his own. One of the works in the image is now astride a granite column marking Lindsay's final resting place in Georgetown, Maine.*

It is through a joint effort that Ilulissat and Uummannaq sustain each other: Ilulissat is in large part a staging area and supply base for transport to, and material goods for, Uummannaq. Each place in its own way welcomes visitors to experience, enjoy, and learn something of this region of Greenland and the Arctic. At one time the Arctic was simply perceived as the top of a globe in the school library. Now it can exist right under one's feet and fill one's eyes with a dramatic beauty that was previously enjoyed by only a few intrepid explorers.

## Arts and Crafts

Arts and crafts as well as music are on the curriculum of the Children's Home. Pierre Auzias, who operates an art studio and sales outlet in Uummannaq (see Chapter 8-Culture), works closely with the children of Uummannaq as well as with artists and collectors in Uummannaq, Nuuk, and Europe. Concerts and

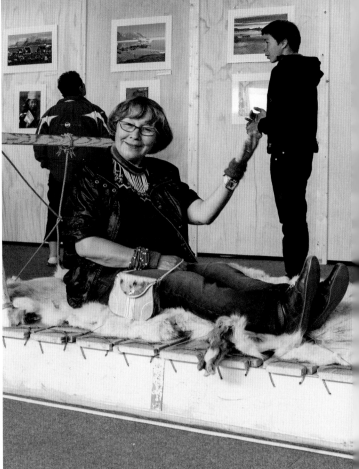

**Show of images by the author**

*In the first image, children at the Uummannaq Community Center watch slides that feature photographs of the polar bear. The second setting, in a former potato shed, features a photo exhibit of images from Greenland and Nunavut. Galleries usually feature a settee or bench of sorts; here it is a sledge, on which the viewer can recline to contemplate the artistry. The sledge is draped with reindeer hides for extra comfort and warmth.*

other celebrations are held at the Children's Home and in the town's public schools and municipal buildings. The community center and art center, both former blubber-storage houses, welcome the public.

As much of my work focuses on Uummannaq, I most appreciate the two exhibitions of my work there and feedback I have received from others who have focused their professional lives on the Arctic. One work of the artist Ap Verheggen (see Chapter 7-Climate Change) is particularly notable. In this work, Verheggen rendered two dog sledges made from metal cable. The sledges were then lifted by helicopter to a drifting iceberg just off shore. The artwork was launched with the hope that it would drift, by wind and current, to Baffin Bay. *Google Earth* tracked progress. Unfortunately, the iceberg had a shorter lifespan than anticipated.

## Kayaking

The recreational activities of kayaking the waters and hiking the land of the Uummannaq region present opportunities for growth. Interest in the indigenous Greenland sea kayak, the sleekest of watercraft (See Chapter 8: Culture), is enjoying a revival, and Greenland has become the place to which Americans and Europeans come to use this type of craft in its original setting. The early 20th Century photograph is of kayakers, with one doing an Eskimo roll.

Four kayakers arrived from Ireland in their own aluminum sailboat in the summer of 2013. Crossing the North Atlantic by sailboat is not that unusual. Working and traveling with the Smithsonian, I have met these particularly hardy travelers not only in Greenland but also in the Gulf of St. Lawrence and Newfoundland. One of these adventurers, who soloed his sailboat from

Norway to Newfoundland by way of Greenland, commented on one danger: cargo containers. Containers that fall off large ships float around like icebergs, partly or fully submerged, and constitute a great threat to small craft navigation.

Stewart and Debbie Roberts, who arrived from Scotland, had their collapsible kayaks and gear shipped from Scotland to Greenland. For two weeks they camped on the islands of Uummannaq Fjord and explored the area in their kayaks. These boats cruise beautifully and provide ample space for gear. Construction is of a light aluminum alloy frame and a skin covering of urethane-coated nylon, and is similar in design and performance to the traditional Greenlandic 'skin on frame' kayak. Both types of boat skim across the water almost effortlessly.

*from top:*
**Eskimo roll**
*In an early twentieth century display of an indigenous skill, a Greenlander rolls his kayak over and up. Image from Knudsen-Holm family archives used with permission.*
**Modern kayakers with fold boats**
*After two weeks of paddling and camping among the islands of Uummannaq Fjord, a Scotsman and his American wife from Chicago pack up their Canadian-made Feathercraft kayaks for shipment back to Scotland.*

Technical climbers, several from Ireland, summited Uummannaq peak. This is a feat that is rarely attempted, let alone achieved (see front cover for a sense of the sheer challenge entailed in such a climb). They had even heard of the International Appalachian Trail (IAT), which was founded in my home state of Maine! A few months later, in the fall of that year (2013), the IAT held its first European meeting, in Scotland, which is a member of the IAT.

*from top:*
**Christmas House with scale**
*Lindsay, at 5ft 3in (1.6m), provides a sense of scale, which shows how small the Christmas House is.*
**Christmas House from a distance**
*Given its low profile and its blend of earthy color and texture, you probably would not see the Christmas House, purportedly where Santa once lived, unless you were looking for it.*

## Christmas House

Towards the northern end of Uummannaq Island, on its west side, is a rare, relatively flat, raised beach on which the Christmas House rests. When I first visited Uummannaq, there was an effort underway to promote Uummannaq as 'Santa's Land'. The story goes that the house was built for a Danish Christmas show. The Christmas House was promoted as Santa's 'real' home. Located on a raised beach with an *inukssuk* on a ridge overlooking this bit of flat rocky land, the Christmas House is diminutive in size, with ceilings under two meters (six feet). Construction of the Christmas House is reportedly based on a standard design for a small, tight, easy-to-heat emergency shelter. The image below, 'Looking Through a Glass Brightly' suggests both the whimsy of nature and the security of the structure.

left to right:
**Christmas motif**
*'Santa and dwarfs' painting and Christmas decorations suggest a year-round Christmas. To obtain an even better gauge of the smallness of structure, note the relative height of chair backs.*
**Christmas House window**
*Windows present some interesting compositions from inside as well as from outside.*

**International Appalachian Trail (IAT) North Greenland**
*In 2009, the establishment of the IAT in Greenland was celebrated in Uummannaq with distribution of IAT-logo hats, pins, vests, and the first IAT group picture in Greenland. In background is the Nuussuaq Peninsula with the mountains where the IAT trail corridor has been located.*

## International Appalachian Trail

In 1994, Richard Anderson of Maine advanced the idea of constructing an International Appalachian Trail (IAT). It would begin in Maine where the U.S. Appalachian Trail has its northern terminus, at Mt. Katahdin. From Mt. Katahdin, it would connect with a trail corridor in the Canadian provinces of Québec and New Brunswick. Since then, chapters have been formed throughout Atlantic Canada, Greenland and on to the Caledonide Mountains of Europe.

**Freeport, Maine—next stop**
*René's crew must first shop for gear at LL Bean.*
**Greenlanders in Maine to climb Mt. Katahdin**
*In 2012, a barbeque is held in the woods behind our home in Georgetown, Maine, for the party of seven Greenlanders who were preparing to climb Mt. Katahdin.*

**Pre-hike photo in Greenland**
*In 2013, our party of 18, with Ann Andreasen standing at right, and Uummannaq in the background, prepare for our Nuussuaq hike.*

In 2009, the northernmost chapter of IAT Greenland was established on the Nuussuaq Peninsula. Establishment of the chapter was sponsored by Ann Andreasen and managed by René Kristensen. The trail traverses the width and length of the peninsula. (Map 3) At about this same time a southern Greenland chapter was established to sponsor existing trails in the south Greenland Narsarsuaq region (Map 1). In 2012, René and five boys from the Children's Home came to Maine to hike the beginning of the International Appalachian Trail, from Mt. Katahdin to the Canadian border at New Brunswick (Also see Chapter 9-Celebrations).

In June of 2013, IAT Greenland, with a hiking party of eighteen staff and students from the Children's Home, one as young as nine, backpacked over the Nuussuaq Peninsula from the Arctic to the 'High Arctic', from Disko Bay to Uummannaq Fjord. There is no real agreement as to the latitude that marks the transition from Arctic to High Arctic because factors of elevation and ocean currents come into play. The transition across Baffin Bay in Nunavut is roughly at 70° while in Uummannaq it is 71°. Given the likelihood that young backpackers would be tired at the end of the trek, a 'south to north' route was selected to have hikers close to home at the end. The trip began by boat to circumnavigate the peninsula from the north side to

the south side, almost to the mainland base of the peninsula
on its south side near the town of Saqqaq. We traveled a distance of
about 300 km (180 mi) by boat. The trek on the IAT back to the north of
Uummannaq Fjord was about 50 km (30 mi) in length.

Despite the cold and snow at 70° north latitude, all completed the 50 km
(30 mi) trek in a week, fording rivers, ascending countless moraines,
climbing mountains, struggling up and down snowfields, and hiking over a
mountain pass of 695m (2,300ft) elevation. Each hiker carried a backpack,
and helped cook and set up the tents. Two of the hikers, Rasmus Alataq and
Kunuunnguaq Knudsen accompanied René on the 2012 hike in Maine

*clockwise from left:*
**Uummannaq flotilla**
*With five boats to carry the hiking party of 18, equipment, food, and five boat drivers, we began a sea voyage of 300km (185mi), which would continue into the next day.*
**Saqqaq**
*We land on the south side of the Nuussuaq peninsula and overnight in Saqqaq. The settlement of Saqqaq is a location where many early artifacts have been found, lending the name 'Saqqaq' to that culture.*

(See Chapter 9-Celebrations). In August of 2016, the Greenland and Maine chapters of the IAT successfully hiked over the Nuussuaq Peninsula.

Geographically, culturally, and environmentally, there is enough experience and adventure offered in Uummannaq Fjord to satisfy the most demanding of travelers. All that is needed is imagination, curiosity, and a love of the north and its mountains—in other words, a spirit attuned to high latitudes and altitudes.

*clockwise from right:*

**Eroded landscape**

*On the second day of our sea journey, we cruised along a landscape with interesting geological features, such as this dyke which is igneous (volcanic) rock extruded in molten form through a fracture in existing even older rock. Rock surrounding the dyke has been eroded.*

**Crossing glacial streams**

*There is an abundance of glacial melt water where long legs and/or a fixed line make streams easier to cross. A fixed line is set at each water crossing.*

**Acclimation**

*It takes some time for young hikers to acclimate to the frigid, raw conditions.*

**A Gateway: the International Appalachian Trail**

*Saqqaq on the northern edge of Disko Bay is a favored jumping off place to pick up the International Appalachian Trail, which traverses north over the Nuussuaq Peninsula to Uummannaq.*

clockwise from top left:

**Descent through snowfields**

*Now on the north side of Nuussuaq Peninsula, the trek is downhill to Uummannaq Fjord.*

**Emergency shelter on ridge**

*Hikers stop to overnight in a shelter that, with some improvising, accommodates all 18 of us. The story is that Knud Rasmussen used this ridge to train his dog team for the Thule Expeditions.*

**Celebratory group photo**

*At the first sight of waters (rather the ice) of Uummannaq, it is time for a group cheer.*

*left to right, from top left:*

**Polar Bear Claw with Carving of Polar Bear**
*by Otto Kilime of Kulusuk, Greenland. 2007. 3".*
**Inuk with Fish**
*by unknown. Soapstone. Baffin Island. Nunavut. Purportedly obtained by father of neighbor Hal Bonner in 1930s. A few years ago, Given to author by Hal's wife Betty Cole. On bottom of sculpture are inscriptions 'E91173' and '1923'. 9" high.*
**Four Faces**
*by Arnie Nielsen. Granite carving. Uummannaq, Greenland. 2015. 14" wide, 13" high.*
**Loon**
*by Mikisiti Saila. Jadeite, Cape Dorset, Nunavut. 2000. 8" x 6".*
**Inuk Face**
*by Cal Best. Moose horn and fossil whale bone. St. Anthony, Newfoundland. 8" wide x 5" high.*
**Small Inuit drum**
*with beads inside. 4" x 8".*
**Eastern Greenlandic Water Drinking Vessel**
*Wood with ivory inlays. Ilulissat, Greenland, 2007. 10" x 5".*
**Faces**
*by Albert Biles (Metis). St. Anthony, Newfoundland. 12" high x 18" wide.*
**Striding Polar Bear**
*by Tommy Takpanic (Inuit). Green and black stone. Kimmirut, Baffin. 2013. 9" long x 5" high.*
**Innu Woman with Child and Man**
*Crows Carvings. Whalebone. Grenfell Mission— St. Anthony, Newfoundland. Base of 3.5" by height of 2.5".*

**King of the Ice**
*by George Collins.*
*Happy Valley / Goose Bay,*
*Labrador. Imported*
*crystalline alabaster with*
*Newfoundland*
*dolomite base. 2005.*
*11" high x 8" wide.*

# Pioneering Science in the Arctic

....[T]entative investigation must of necessity prove incomplete in many respects, and in other respects incorrect. All the same it must be ventured. For once the major considerations have been established, it will not be difficult, through detailed investigations, to eliminate errors.

*Mott T. Greene. Alfred Wegener: Science, Exploration and the Theory of Continental Drift (2015, 265).*

Science advances through a back-and-forth movement between supposition, theory, fieldwork, and experimentation. Given the arduous demands of Arctic climes, truth to be discovered or recognized requires dedication, time, and discomfort to the point of misery, injury, even death. Bit-by-bit, science advances. Yet, as a consequence of the modern Agricultural and Industrial Revolutions, most human cultures have contemporaneously lost their millennially gained intimate linkage to their surroundings, that is, knowledge, of people and place. The one notable exception remains the people of the high north where neither of these revolutions could occur nor be transplanted (Ruddiman 2005, UNESCO 2009, Bolster 2012). These Arctic peoples are repositories of ancient ways of knowledge, of judgment in reading the landscape, and of a culture with prehistoric roots that prevails even in Earth's most challenging ecosystem, the Arctic, from Siberia to Greenland (Map 1).

Knowledge of ancient ways has been gleaned through the archeological study of ancient cultures. Arctic archeology has important roots in northern Greenland where settlement began more than four thousand years ago with the Independence I culture. A settlement on the south side of Nuussuaq Peninsula has been named 'Saqqaq' after the town where these artifacts were found at that location (Fitzhugh 2015, Schledermann 1996).

In the early decades of the twentieth century in this region of Greenland, archaeologists and climatologists pioneered methodological advances in fieldwork while working in the challenging circumstances of a polar climate. Three names are associated with advancements in these embryonic fields of science—archaeologists Therkel Mathiassen, a Dane, Frederica de Laguna, an American, and climatologist and meteorologist Alfred Wegener, a German. Wegener is known as the 'Father of Plate Tectonics', a theory that explains continental drift (1924). The framework of this chapter combines a consideration of Eskimo cultural evolution and the work of these three contemporary field scientists who carefully studied culture and climate in the early twentieth century in the Uummannaq/Upernavik region. I add my own observations of the land to celebrate their work.

## Archaeology

For years scientists have been aware of different rhythms of life in the Arctic….[C]hanges in the composition of arctic plant communities have occurred periodically with a change in climate….A careful examination of arctic refuse middens…has revealed a succession of differently equipped early human cultures, whose entries into the Arctic are also related to periods of climate change. (Lopez 1987 (1986), 155)

## Polar Geography

Fitzhugh writes of a Paleo-Eskimo culture not well studied because of its spatial spread across this continent-size island, with implications for different climates by region, "separated by great differences and physical barriers." Greenland's latitude extends some 23° [2,600km (1,600mi) south to north]. Given this range, Greenland's environments vary greatly in ecological complexity and productivity, ranging from Peary Land's High Arctic deserts and permanently frozen coasts to its 'Scandinavian' subarctic regions (Fitzhugh 1984, 528). Thus, any cultural generalizations of this ice-covered and mountainous island continent, where migration is limited only to its periphery, are limited.

The environment of west Greenland, where the sea is ice-free many months of the year and the fauna is relatively more diverse, offers greater opportunity for human settlement than does north or east Greenland. An important cultural factor is that Greenland has only one point of contact to enable land migration—High Arctic Canada. For polar migrations, which began in Siberia, Greenland is the physical terminus for Paleo-Eskimo, Neo-Eskimo, and Inuit cultures. Richard Jordan writes: "[W] ith a gateway in the High Arctic accessible to only those cultures adapted to its harshest extremes, Greenland has the potential of being a population trap far removed from the origin place of Eskimo societies 1,500 miles to the west in the Bering Sea region (1984, 538-539)."

Table 6-1 presents a timeline, for north and west Greenland, for the cultural progression from Paleo-Eskimo Independence I and II to Saqqaq to Neo-Eskimo Thule, and modern Greenland. By 4,500 BP (before present) glacial ice had disappeared from the central Canadian Arctic. Warm climate and ice-free summer waters helped Paleo-Eskimos expand from Alaska as far east as Greenland, becoming known as the Independence I or Pre-Dorset (in Canada) culture. Shortly afterward, about 4,000 BP, a different Paleo-Eskimo culture, known as Saqqaq, was established in west Greenland. This was followed by the Dorset culture, around 2,000 BP (Fitzhugh and Richard 2014, Fitzhugh 1984, Gulløv 2004). The Uummannaq and Upernavik regions both had Paleo-Eskimo Saqqaq and Dorset cultures.

## Table 6-1. North and West Greenland Cultures Preceding Western Contact, Before Present (BP)

|  | Name | Date (BP) |
|---|---|---|
| **North** | Independence I* | 4300 – 3800 |
|  | Independence II | 3800 – 2500 |
|  | Thule | 700 – 500 |
|  |  |  |
| **West** | Independence I | 4300 – 3800 |
|  | Saqqaq/Sarqaq | 3600 – 3000 |
|  | Independence II | 3800 – 2500 |
|  | Dorset | 2000 – 1500 |
|  | Thule | 700 – 500 |
|  | Inugssuk/Inugsuk/Inussuk | 500 – 300 |
|  | Greenlandic Inuit** | 300 AD to present |

\* *The Independence Culture is named after Independence Fjord, which is located in northeast Greenland.*

\*\* *Indigenous people of Greenland refer to themselves as 'Greenlandic' and to their cousins on the other side of Baffin Bay as 'Inuit'. There remains some debate regarding the acceptance of this classification.*

A new culture began to arrive in the eastern Arctic around 1250 AD—1300 AD. This Neo-Eskimo or Thule traditional culture is named for an archaeological site at Thule in northwest Greenland (a term derived from the ancient Greeks meaning the most northern part of the world), settled by a people who had learned to hunt large whales around the Bering Strait. With a then warm climate, Thule whale-hunters moved swiftly across Canada into northern Greenland. By this time the Norse had established colonies in Greenland. Later Thule culture came into contact with the Norse and transitioned to the Inugssuk culture. Thule and their Inugssuk successors were a technically complex and advanced culture equipped with sledge dogs, kayaks, umiaks, bow and arrow, large skin-covered whaling boats, and toggling harpoons.

## Knud Rasmussen and the Thule Expeditions

If there is one figure in Greenlandic history who has earned the right to be known as the 'Father of Greenland', it is Knud Rasmussen. Rasmussen was born in then Jakobshavn (Ilulissat), Greenland, of a Danish vicar and a mother who was born a Fleischer. Knud's mother was an ancestor of Kunuunnguaq Fleischer, (then of Uummannaq) whom I met in Uummannaq at a *kaffemik*—birthday party—for his wife Naja Rosing, also a significant name in Greenlandic history.

In 1910, with his friend Peter Freuchen (godfather to Inger Knudsen's sister Helga), these two Danes, both fluent in the Greenlandic version of Inuktitut, established the Thule Trading Station, which served as a trading post for the *Inughuit*, or Polar Inuit living in the Thule District of North Greenland. This source of financial support provided for a series of seven expeditions between 1912 and 1933, known as the Thule Expeditions (Table 6-2). Freuchen, an anthropologist and famous novelist, was an expedition member and also a frequent advisor on Greenland to German climatologist Alfred Wegener (Greene 2015, 144-148, 541, 542, 558, 559).

In the Thule Expeditions, Rasmussen "…saw a great loss of freedom in the new world order, in the progression from traditional societies to market societies, and perhaps a crushing of the spirit." Rasmussen "…could tell when they were nearing a trading post, as he saw the evidence on display in the villages: wool blankets instead of caribou hides, ironware instead of carved and polished driftwood or stone, aluminum and tin instead of soapstone (240)." In summation of Rasmussen's life's work: "No one else could have accomplished what Rasmussen did….Although not considered 'scientific,' his ethnographic collections are a priceless contribution to world culture…" (Brown, 2015: 35, 179).

## Table 6-2: The Thule Expeditions

| | |
|---|---|
| **1912** | The First Thule Expedition with Rasmussen and Freuchen, set forth to disprove the American Robert Peary's claim that a channel divided Peary Land from Greenland, making possible a U.S. territorial claim. In this, Rasmussen and Freuchen succeeded (Freuchen 1953). |
| **1916–1918** | The Second Thule Expedition mapped Greenland's little-known north coast. |
| **1919** | The Third Thule Expedition laid supplies for Amundsen's polar expedition. |
| **1919–1920** | The Fourth Thule Expedition conducted in east Greenland, collected ethnographic information from the Tunumiit, one of Greenland's distinct Inuit cultures. |
| **1921–1924** | The Fifth Thule Expedition with 20,000 miles traveled by expedition members, was the most comprehensive and exhaustive Arctic travel Rasmussen was to undertake. The journey was from Greenland through Arctic Canada and Alaska, to Siberia where he was denied a continuation of his ethnographic studies. With copious information gathered through ethnography, narrative, and archaeology, he was able to address the question known as 'The Eskimo Problem', the origins of the early Eskimo cultures. (Fitzhugh 2016, 28) |
| **1931** **1933** | Rasmussen conducted the Sixth (1931) and Seventh (1933) expeditions. On the last expedition, he was stricken with botulism from eating *kiviaq*, which consists of little auks fermented in the hollowed out skin and blubber of a flensed seal. After extended time and travel by water from east Greenland to Nuuk and then onto Copenhagen, he passed away from a combination of botulism, influenza, and pneumonia. |

*Rasmussen 1927, 1999; Encyclopedia Britannica*, Thule Archives—Book of Days Tales

## Inugssuk culture

The Inugssuk, a hybrid culture that materialized in west Greenland, reflected the influence of trade with the Norse and the use of materials scavenged from abandoned Norse sites. The waters of west Greenland were ice-free during the warm climate of the Medieval Warm Period. This created an environment more favorable and more faunally diverse, and with greater opportunities for human settlement than in north Greenland with its frigid waters from the Arctic Ocean. On both land and water, these people were highly mobile and "had a flexible social organization that readily fragmented into small colonizing groups during expansionary periods." (Jordan 1984, 540)

Jordan, quoting Mathiassen, observes that

> *Data from excavation of Eskimo houses and middens at Inugsuk ...first led Therkel Mathiassen (1931a: 275) to define the Inugsuk culture as "a special Greenland culture ...closely related to the Thule culture and a further development of it"... Inugsuk culture must be looked upon as a phase of the Thule culture influenced by mediaeval Norse culture." (1984, 544)*

Jordan continues:

> *It is almost certain...that Neo-Eskimo groups occupied more northerly regions of west Greenland at an earlier time. Norse artifacts in Eskimo sites with harpoon forms that are older in the Thule District than in west Greenland indicate that Eskimo expansion across Melville Bay probably occurred about AD 1200 and spread at least as far south as Disko Bay." (1984, 544)*

Through the Norse sagas, Jordon provides further credence to the likelihood of interaction between Norse and Eskimo:

> *Norse sagas suggest this area [Disko Bay] was part of their northern hunting grounds, called the Nordrseta. Given the poor chronological placement of most west Greenland Inugsuk sites, it is not yet possible to decide whether Norse artifacts in Eskimo middens result from trading or raiding or whether they were obtained from Norse sites after abandonment. (1984, 54)*

With reference to the success of Inugssuk culture, Fitzhugh observes, as did Mathiassen (1927, 1931a, 1931b), that

> *...[W]here biological production and the forces of physical attrition are delicately balanced, a small human population might live frugally for only a short period before their consumption out-stripped the regenerative capacities of land and sea. ...extinction or emigration followed by a subsequent short fallow period is necessary before new colonization can occur. (1984, 528)*

As I discuss below, it was the fieldwork of Mathiassen and later de Laguna in 1929-1930 in the Upernavik region that first recognized the Inugssuk culture. Inugssuk culture expanded south from Upernavik-Disko into the Norse areas of SW Greenland about 1400 AD. Inugssuk culture was distinguished by an increased dependence on hunting by means of kayak, umiak, and dog-drawn sledges.

*Encyclopedia Britannica* reports the discovery of artifacts that show Norse influence or contact, such as small wooden containers produced by the coopering technique, and trade goods such as church-bell metal and woven wool cloth. Inugssuk culture spread southward along the west coast of Greenland to its southern tip and then moved northward along the east coast. In northeastern Greenland Inugssuk mixed with earlier cultural elements, forming the hybrid northeast Greenland mixed culture. (http://www.britannica.com/topic/Inugsuk-culture)

## Therkel Mathiassen and Frederica de Laguna

The archaeological discoveries of northern Greenland include Comer's kitchen midden in the area of Qaanaaq that was discovered by Captain John Comer of the US in 1916. Later, when Mathiassen excavated the Thule site in Naujan, in northwestern Hudson Bay while on the Fifth Thule Expedition, he recognized its distinctive artifacts as similar to those from Comer's midden in Thule, Greenland, and coined the term 'Thule' for this widespread culture.

Mathiassen's international fame came with his exploration of Thule Culture as part of Knud Rasmussen's Fifth Danish Thule Expedition (1921–1924), in the process establishing Danish leadership of the new field of Eskimology. The great question of archaeology at the time was 'The Eskimo Problem,' determining whether Eskimos originated from Canadian Indians, Siberia or Alaska. (Fitzhugh 2016, 166)

With their colony Greenland as a research base, Danes were to develop the early field techniques for Arctic archaeology. Later, with World II, the establishment of U.S. air bases and of the Cold War's DEW line, the support of Arctic studies was enhanced through access to military infrastructure. Many of my own trips to Greenland are by way of the US National Science Foundation's access to military C-130 flights from the Scotia, New York air base to Kangerlussuaq on Søndrestrom Fjord. I was fortunate to have secured assistance from Danes who placed me in contact with the U.S. National Science Foundation for flights to Greenland.

**Nuugaarsuk landscape**
*Bedrock with scattered erratics is a common sight
in High Arctic lands. Settlements arrayed along the
edge of the sea depend on the sea for food.*

In 1929 Therkel Mathiassen began site excavation on the island of
Inugssuk, within what had been the District of Upernavik, located just to the
north of Uummannaq Fjord (Mathiassen 1930, Holtved 1944, Collins 1946).
About 20km (12mi) due north of Upernavik and 3km (2mi) east from
Kingittorsuaq Island (72° 56' 59.33"N; 56° 06' 59.45"W), Inugssuk is a small
island at the northwestern end, and the south side of Upernavik Icefjord.
Arctic anthropologist Frederica de Laguna tells of an Eskimo story that
"In olden times Norsemen lived on Inugsuk…" (1977, 35). In 1929, on her
first field experience in the Arctic, de Laguna worked with Danish archaeolo-
gist Therkel Mathiassen on Inugssuk. In 2007 while my wife Lindsay and
I were visiting Upernavik, resident Eskimologist Bo Albrechtsen took us on a
boat tour to the south side of the Upernavik Ice Fjord to an island near
Inugssuk, which was identified by Bo as Nuugaarsuk (72° 46.74' N;
55° 35.15'W).

Frederica de Laguna, who became Mathiassen's field assistant, began
her association with anthropology, along with Margaret Mead and
Ruth Benedict as fellow students at Columbia University in New York
City under the mentorship of Franz Boas, the 'Father of American
Anthropology.' In a summation of de Laguna's professional life as
anthropologist, Fitzhugh writes:

> *De Laguna is probably the last American scholar to live through the twentieth
> century as a quintessential Boasian four-field anthropologist [archaeology,
> cultural anthropology, physical anthropology, linguistics]…. [Later] cultural
> investigations were done more and more by teams of specialists, making the
> Boasian generalist a rare, if not obsolete phenomenon. (2016, 232)*

De Laguna's report (1977) on her work with Mathiassen and Inugssuk provides a vivid description of this culture and the cultural implications of indigenous artifacts found there. These Thule ruins are located near Inugssuk (72° 57' N; 56° 06'W). In 1929, Frederica de Laguna (nicknamed 'Freddy'), a then promising archaeologist, had her first Arctic field experience. It was to be a 'Medieval Eskimo' (Inugssuk) dig on Inugssuk Island, located just north of Uummannaq Fjord in the Upernavik Archipelago. De Laguna was very much an astute observer of Greenland. She saw the dig site as within a barren desert: "From a little distance any Greenland coast looks like a desert, for the scanty vegetation makes but a poor show among the rocks...." (de Laguna 1977, 206). I, too, have often observed and written of the desert-like qualities of Greenland. Almost a century later, as ice melt accelerates, on a sunny day the coastal mountains of this section of Greenland could be mistaken for the landscape of Arizona or New Mexico.

De Laguna saw the Arctic as her promised land. Full of wonder and surprise, she felt at home and a part of the Arctic. Quoting from her diary many decades later, "I feel as if I have never been alive before... I am in Greenland: it's really myself here..." (de Laguna 1977, 101), and she says that her life was learning how to live on "...the happy dirt of primitive life." (de Laguna 1977, 109)

She had never done anything like this before. She even terminated her engagement to an Englishman, and instead, falls in love with archaeology, Greenland, and maybe also Dr. Therkel Mathiassen, who was unusually enlightened because females then were not often permitted on excavations. In time she was accepted. Upon being asked if Freddy was a servant, Mathiassen responded, "she is an *agbara* (comrade)." (de Laguna 1977, 220)

The image on page 85 is of a Nuugaarsuk landscape, a typical view of the islands within the Upernavik Archipelago. The stone lintel above the entrance characterizes the innovative design of a Thule house (de Laguna 1977, 112; also see Fitzhugh and Richard 2014, 234). On Inugssuk, the Mathiassen party uncovered a wooden Eskimo doll, which had Norse characteristics resembling either a Norseman or woman "since the style of dress was very similar for both sexes.... It was of the same style as men's dresses in Norway between the twelfth and the middle of the fourteenth century." (de Laguna 1977, 181)

Another set of artifacts found on Inugssuk led Mathiassen to conclude, "...The Inugssuk Eskimo must have learned from the Norsemen." Tubs and pails were patterned after those of the Norse: "[It] is significant that it is only in Greenland, where they had a chance to learn from the Norsemen, that they mastered the principle of coopering." (de Laguna 1977, 184-185) Both Norse and Thule occupied this region of Greenland, which we now know as Upernavik, by the 13th Century. The Inuit proved culturally adept at assimilating Norse technology and material goods, removing cultural materials from their original context, in the process creating a third culture. Examples include duplication of Norse carvings, or use of metal from church bells and other Norse cultural detritus to produce, for example, saws and knives, and the adoption of 'elaborate scroll carving of the Norsemen'. (de Laguna 1977, 182)

Yet another example of cultural borrowing, identified by Danish archaeologist Eigil Knuth in 1947 in northeastern Greenland's Peary Land, was the wooden frame of a 10.5m (33ft) umiak that he concluded had been sailed north around Greenland, presumably when less severe ice conditions allowed limited near-shore navigation. The radiocarbon age of this umiak, about 650 BP, included an oak member and iron nails in its construction, indicating that its Inuit builders had had contact with Norse settlers on the west coast of Greenland, likely a site in the Upernavik Archipelago. On this same expedition, Knuth, at Independence Fjord, discovered stone tent rings of two distinct Inuit cultures that had migrated from Canada's Ellesmere Island across Smith Sound to the east edge of northern Greenland (roughly 82° N; 27° W). He named these two migratory waves Independence I—likely a proto-Saqqaq culture, and Independence II—an early Dorset culture. The two cultures are separated by almost two millennia. (Fitzhugh 1984)

Frederica de Laguna had a passionate love for archaeology. She had a real gift for presenting detail in her everyday work, a hallmark throughout her career as archaeologist, and later, as an ethnologist. She particularly loved archaeology in northern landscapes, regardless of the cold, ice, water, and mud. Eventually, she moved the geographic focus of her fieldwork from Greenland to America's Arctic, Alaska, where she continued her fieldwork. Through her pioneering efforts, Denmark and the United States have solidly established archaeology as a science in both Greenland and Alaska. One also admires the courage and endurance of these scientists as they dealt with a hostile climate: snow, ice, mud, and mosquitoes. There were no well-protected, heated indoor locations for their research.


## Exploring Ancient Uummannaq Fjord

My travels in the region, for more than a decade, included visits to several archeological sites with René Kristensen or my wife Lindsay. Our rule on these visits was to move nothing, and to take only photographs. Little actual digging has occurred for some time at the sites we visited, including Uummannaq, Storøen, Qaarsut, Qilakitsoq, Issua on Telerua Island, Nuussuaq Bear Trap, and the Upernavik Archipelago. It is helpful at this point to digress for a moment to describe various man-made structures made of rock.

**Inukssuk as signage**
*An inukssuk guides the traveler over land and serves as a navigation aid visible from the sea. From the tallest to the shortest, they serve as markers that endure Arctic weather. Requiring no maintenance, they literally stand the test of time.*

## Inuksuit and the Burial Cairns

Like other Arctic regions where soil is either thin or non-existent, cultural remains often appear as an arrangement of rocks, for example as a vertical inukssuk ('like a man'), as animal traps, turf and stone housing, or dome-like burial mounds. The primary archaeological features of indigenous Green-landers are two: the inukssuk and the burial cairn. Both are made of rock. An *inukssuk* (*inuksuit*—plural) means, "…that which acts in the capacity of a human" (Hallendy 2000, 203). Rasmussen speaks of cairns as "monuments erected to the memory of the dead". The root Inuk means man. Inuksuit appear throughout the Arctic variously indicating land routes, maritime mark-ers visible from the sea, food caches, a good place to hunt, or sometimes simply for companionship (Hallendy 2000, 22). The large inukssuk shown above towers three to four meters tall on a hill over the settlement of Qaarsut. Com-pare that with a diminutive 'less-than-knee high' inukssuk on the ridge behind the settlement of Nuugaatsiaq. Viewed from a ridge, overlooking raised beach, a meter-plus inuksuk of stacked rocks marks a landing site for sea voyagers.

Traditional burial cairns are not found in a Christian cemetery; rather, they are located near old campsites or villages and frequently on hillsides or on prominent landmark features. Burial cairns and inuksuit are primarily artifacts of the Thule and Inugssuk cultures. A notable exception in Uummannaq

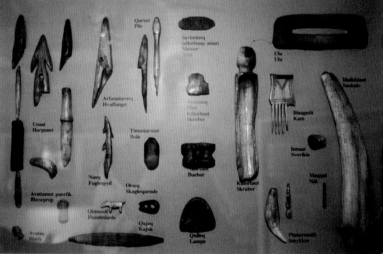

from top:

**Umiaq, the 'women's boat'**

*The Greenlandic cultural display, part of Uummannaq's
250th anniversary in 2013, included a restored umiaq.*

**Thule artifacts**

*As seen here, displays in the Uummannaq Museum
are from the Dorset, Saqqaq, and Thule cultures.*

**Framing an umiaq**

*The skeleton of this large sturdy boat, fashioned from
scavenged wood and bone, is under construction in the
early twentieth century. Image from Knudsen-Holm
family archives used with permission.*

**Women aboard an umiaq**
*The umiak is a vessel large enough to carry all the family's hunting, fishing, and household goods, a job unsuited to the smaller sleeker kayak. Image from Knudsen-Holm family archives used with permission.*

Fjord is Qilakitsoq, early fifteenth century mummies intered beneath the shelter of a ledge overhang, before Columbus visited the Americas; they are now exhibited in the National Museum of Greenland in Nuuk. The rocky substrate of Greenland makes interment below ground difficult, and of necessity burials are above ground in cairn graves. Christian burials in Greenland are placed in the ground in cemeteries with stone or wood markers. Cairn graves may last indefinitely and reveal the extent of Inuit populations in all regions they occupied.

## Uummannaq

Located up the slope in Uummannaq is the Uummannaq Museum, which has an extensive collection of Saqqaq and Thule artifacts, a recent display included an *umiaq*, a large 'women's boat' made from skin over a frame of driftwood. From a contemporary perspective, while there has been renewed interest in the kayak, this is not true for the umiaq. In the Knudsen-Holm family collection of photographs is one image made by an unknown photographer at the turn of the twentieth century in northwest Greenland showing an umiak frame being assembled that will then be covered with sealskins. Another image shows Inuit women with their distinctive topknot hairstyle boarding an umiaq, perhaps to visit family or friends in another settlement.

Kunuunnguaq Fleischer put Lindsay and me in contact with Uummannaq's then Municipal Engineer, Niels Mønsted, an avid rock hound who explores the islands and mainland of this west/northwest section of Greenland. His wife, Lucia Ludvigsen, was operating their home as a bed and breakfast. He was associated with the tourism sector and for a time was curator of the Uummannaq Museum. Lucia was listed in *Iceland, Greenland, & the Faroe Islands* (Lonely Planet Publications), also as an organizer of boat and dog sledge trips (Cornwallis and Swaney 2001).

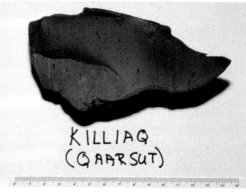

**Burial Site**
*Niels Mønsted points out a human skull visible within a disintegrating burial mound.*
**Artifacts**
*A scraper made of Killiaq, a kind of slate from the Nuussuaq Peninsula.*

KILLIAQ
(QAARSUT)

During an early visit to the west side of Uummannaq Island with Lucia and Niels, the wind blew from the south and surf was running high. Ice was shoved around the pontoon dock that is used for smaller boats. Traveling among growler-size icebergs, we motored north in a small fishing boat along the west side of Uummannaq Island. On landing at a raised beach, we almost immediately found chips of gray Killiaq flint that originates in Qaarsut, where a tall inukssuk overlooks an old village site whose houses measure about 7m x 8m (23ft x 26ft), accompanied by four raised stone grave mounds and a gushing stream of cold, crystal-clear, water. Generations have used this site for berrying, sealing, fishing, socializing, and for preserving food obtained by hunting, fishing, and gathering. As seen by contemporary-style table and chairs made of rock, along with a halibut smoker, the site with charcoal and food remnants had signs of still being in use.

## Storøen

The following day we accompanied Niels and Lucia to Storøen Island, immediately to the east of Uummannaq. Storøen is Danish for 'the big island'; the Greenlandic name is *Sageliaruseq*, 'the island behind.' Names often supply geographical information for finding one's way. With heavy fog, the weather was not the best for water travel although shafts of sunlight occasionally pierced the clouds. The site on Storøen is just beyond a sheer rock face that commands the western end of the island and rises to 1350m (4400ft) above sea level, with another 1,000m (3,300ft) extending below sea level. Here there is a turf house and seven burial cairns—five of stone and

**Habitations marked by stone**
*With Qaarsut airport in the background we have a juxtaposition of two cultures, one perhaps ancient and indigenous, the other modern and western.*

two a mix of driftwood and stone. The presence of wood indicates the arrival of Christianity and its practice of burial in a rectangular wooden box instead of the use of traditional reindeer clothing and burial in a cairn. We also found Killiaq flint eroding at the sea's edge.

## Qaarsut

Over the years, we have made a number of visits to Qaarsut. In an early visit, I met school headmaster Esben Christensen. Lindsay and I explored moraines and outwash from the ice in the glaciers behind the settlement. While looking for Killiaq flint we came across a turf dwelling—Saqqaq culture perhaps—which had been reduced to its base of stonewalls. Other stone structures continued up to the hills behind the airport where the only locally known source of Killiaq flint has been located (Sørensen and Buck Pedersen, 2005). The airport is clearly visible about two miles to the east.

While there, Esben shared his belief that weather in Greenland has become more like that of Denmark, as caused by evaporation of warmer water that then condenses as fog. Once the weather cleared, I walked towards the Killiaq site at the airport. As I started walking I found a turf house between the road and the sea. The house measured approximately 5m x 7m (16ft x 23ft) and is next to a stream. Airport fuel tanks that dominate the scene are in the background. At another turf house on the other side of the stream, I found what appeared to be a polar bear tooth and also a burial site where the

**Qilakitsoq**
*Qilakitsoq establishes a physical presence on the skyline that renders the site visible from Uummannaq. With reference to this image, the location of the mummified 15th century Inuit remains is behind the viewer.*

remains had been dug up, probably by dogs. The site is alongside the road and close to two long houses at the end of the village: ancient building stones and recent airport tarmac co-exist.

I walked to the airport with the thought of going into hills behind the airport terminal, but visibility again dropped to zero: the runway is by the sea at only 100m (330ft) elevation, with the cloud floor right on the tarmac. Along the road to the airport are turf houses that predate the road. The airport and village road must have been constructed over an indigenous, travel corridor.

## Qilakitsoq

With an invitation from Ann Andreasen, we were underway to the 'mummy place' at Qilakitsoq, meaning 'where the land touches the sky' (Hart Hansen, *et al*, 1985, 1991). We went to the waterfront in Qaarsut to be picked up by a boat to Qilakitsoq. While Lindsay, Esben and I were waiting, the face of a nearby iceberg calved into the sea, causing a threatening swell of water to tilt up the pontoon float on which we were standing. We rushed up the embankment so as not to get swamped by icy water. A concerned hunter rushed to the float to rescue a freshly killed seal that was tied there.

When an open fishing boat piloted by Simion Løvstrøm arrived, we left for Qilakitsoq, just down the coast from Qaarsut and across from the island of Uummannaq on the Nuussuaq Peninsula (Map 3). This is the place where, in 1972, while hunting, two brothers, Hans and Jokum Grønvold, discovered the well-preserved bodies of seven women and children. Our trip was cold and windy, and there were many icebergs requiring Simion to make frequent course corrections. The approach to Qilakitsoq was particularly congested with ice.

As we approached the landing place, we were greeted by a group of eight visitors at the site who were having an impromptu reception with crackers, cheese, and sweets. Everyone, with the exception of the on-site master of ceremonies, Birthe Pedersen, was 'from away'. On this cold, dark day,

*from top:*
**Hans Grønvold**
*At the home of mutual friend Pierre Auzias in 2012. Hans tells the fascinating story of how 40 years earlier, he and his brother, while hunting, discovered the long-preserved bodies of women and children.*
**Lower level burials**
*Separate from the 'mummy' burial place, these burials are more contemporary than those of the 15th century burials treated below.*

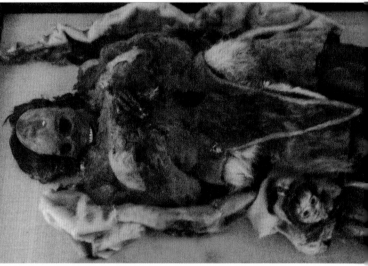

*from top:*
**Burial chamber**
*One of the two shaft-like chambers where mummies were exhumed, in 1978. (See Hansen, Meldgaard, Nordqvist, 1991. Figure 31, p.47)*
**National Museum of Greenland—Mummies**
*The remarkable preservation of the mummies is seen in the delicacy of the woman's hands, and we are drawn to the lifelike qualities of the baby's face.*

one visitor from Nuuk wore a topcoat, tie, and street loafers. After being warmly welcomed, we hiked further up to view the burial place. Later, I was introduced to *Gammel Dansk*, or 'Old Dane', a liquor tasting like the Maine carbonated, non-alcoholic beverage '*Moxie*'. Both are acquired tastes. On this, the lower level of the site, are many cairn burials that have become carpeted with a thick layer of vegetation.

The seven mummies found here had been moved to the National Museum of Greenland, where we viewed them on a later visit to Nuuk. These bodies were first interred in the mid-fifteenth century, about a half-century before Columbus made his way to the Western Hemisphere. Since removal from Qilakitsoq, the mummies and their fur clothing have undergone state-of-the-art restoration. Particularly striking is an infant, with long expressive eyelashes, resting on the arm of a woman with graceful hands; she wears finely restored reindeer (*Rangifer tarandus*) clothing. Much has changed over the past five centuries in our world while these mummies rested in two narrow shafts, protected from precipitation and cold by a cliff overhang.

*clockwise from top:*

**Raised beach**
*With Nuussuaq Peninsula in the background, this site, known as 'Isua,' possesses a gentle sloping shoreline and flat land, facilitating either temporary or longer habitation.*

**Sheltered cook area**
*The soot-covered overhang is large enough to protect the area for cooking and to provide shelter from the elements.*

**René peers into a burial cairn**

**Burial cairns**
*Three cairns are seen on a relatively high ridge above the site's raised beach.*

**Humans and muskox**
*The contents of these cairns are both human and muskox (Ovibos moschatus). In some burials muskox is used as a burial shroud, while other burials appear to be a depository for both human and muskox remains. Remains in this image include two human skeletons.*

## Issua Settlement on Telerua

Issua is on the small island of Telerua, located between Ikerasak Island and the Nuussuaq Peninsula (Map 3). Though long abandoned, Issua is characterized by remnants of turf houses, places for food caches, and at least six domelike burial cairns on or near a ridge. René and I photographed the interiors through small crevices that have opened up in the domes. The contents included human skeletons, fur clothing, and what appeared to be muskox (*Ovibos moschatus*) remains, mingling with humans in death as they do in life. A nearby raised beach could have provided access, living space, and an overhang under which to cook. Burial cairns appeared on rises, some alone and some in groups. All interiors held human remains (some cairns held more than one skeleton), clothing, and muskox remains. Jorgen Dahl, a Dane who has lived in Ikerasak for a half-century as caretaker of a Children's Home outreach residence facility, describes an Inuit burial site as being placed high so as to be closer to the nothingness of space where all begins, and ends. The Inuit burial cairns lie in contrast to the newer Christian cemetery, marked by an array of wooden crosses, which is found in the settlement of Ikerasak.

## Nuussuaq Bear Trap and Beyond to Upernavik Archipelago

At the tip of Nuussuaq Peninsula, the abandoned settlement of Nuussuaq (Map 3) dramatically juts into the frigid, desolate, windblown Arctic waters of Baffin Bay. It affords a somewhat weather-protected site from which to observe a broad expanse of northern waters. Here is located a time-etched but solid stonewalled structure with a ground level entrance, locally referred to as the 'Bear Trap'. There is doubt, however, whether this structure could

**Nuussuaq Bear Trap**
*Scattered flat rocks in the foreground indicate that the bear trap has diminished in size through either human activity or the forces of nature. For scale, note head of René Kristensen behind the structure. The bear trap is about two meters in depth.*

**Tip of Nuussuaq Peninsula**
*For the Norse and for others who may have followed, this site overlooking Baffin Bay would have been an excellent observation point for game and potential enemies.*

actually contain a polar bear (*Ursus maritimus*), especially one enraged by entrapment. Since the Norse visited this area each spring, there is little doubt that they built the 'bear trap.' During the first half of the second millennium, the Norse sailed here from their settlements in southern Greenland (Map 1), roughly from as far away as Narsaq, to hunt narwhal (*Monodon monoceros*), walrus (*Odobenus rosmarus*), and polar bear. The Norsemen hunted these animals for ivory and furs to satisfy tithing requirements of church and crown.

The first solid evidence of Norse voyages north from Vesterbygd, the Norse Western Settlement, are clearly indicated by a Norse rune stone message, dated between 1250 AD and 1350 AD, found in 1824 on Kingittorsuaq Island (72° 57. 36' N; 56° 13.39' W) in the Upernavik Archipelago. On that small, rectangular stone, three Norse names are recorded commemorating the forthcoming Rogation Day, celebrated on April 25 and including a prayer to avoid calamities. Schledermann believes that 1250 AD marked the first landing by 'pioneering Thule Inuit families' who crossed from Canada's Ellesmere Island and down the west coast of Greenland (1996, 124).

## Twenty-first Century Burials

In 2009, upon arriving from Copenhagen for our first Christmas in the Arctic, Lindsay and I were told of the death of a staff member of the Children's Home. Although outsiders, we were invited to attend the church service. After the funeral service on December 21, which included a hymn composed by a Greenlander, we were invited to participate in the burial ceremony. In a procession from the hospital, a pickup truck carried the casket and led the procession to a cemetery on the outskirts of town. A simple wooden cross carried the name of the deceased. Near the grave, newly excavated by drill and blasting, many candles flickered in the cold December wind. Later, all present slowly returned to town.

**Funeral service**
*Service ends and the deceased continues her passage.*
**Passage to interment**
*Men of Uummannaq, dressed in traditional clothing, bear the deceased. A slow procession wound its way along the water's edge and out of town to the cemetery. Friends and relatives offer their last words before burial.*
**Burial site of Navarana**
*Wife of Peter Freuchen, they met and married in Thule. Navarana had accompanied Freuchen on one of the Thule Expeditions. As she had not been baptized a Christian, the vicar at Upernavik forbid her burial on hallowed ground but Freuchen prevailed.*

An earlier interment, one that became famous, was that of Inughuit (northern Greenlander) Navarana, first wife of Peter Freuchen and mother of his two children. She died from the Spanish Flu in 1921 and was buried in Upernavik, then the northern extreme of Danish colonial rule.

## Climatology

### Alfred Wegener and Continental Drift

> *Wegener's idea—that the continents move—is at the heart of the theory that guides the earth sciences today: plate tectonics. This theory is in many respects quite different from Wegener's proposal, in the same way that modern evolutionary theory is very different from Darwin's original ideas about biological evolution. Yet plate tectonics is a descendant of Alfred Wegener's theory of continental drift, in quite the same way that modern evolutionary theory is a descendant of Darwin's theory of natural selection. (Greene 2015, Preface ix)*

In the early years of the twentieth century, archaeology earned its spurs as a science. Simultaneously, and largely through government and university support, climatology—the study of weather (as a branch of meteorology, the study of atmosphere)—was also becoming established. As it happened, both archaeology and climatology shared the same geographical venue—Greenland, and even some of the same personalities: Peter Freuchen and Knud Rasmussen. Significantly, it was through the Danes and the Germans in Uummannaq that climatology became an advanced field science.

Alfred Wegener was a scientist dedicated to Greenland, where much of his scientific work was conducted and where he died, in 1930, on the ice cap. History does not remember Wegener so much as an Arctic explorer than as a scientist who articulated the Theory of Continental Drift. In his meticulously written biography of Wegener, over 25 years in the making, Professor of Earth and Space Sciences Mott Greene details Wegener's life as an ingenious theoretician, a multidisciplinary field scientist, and sagacious Arctic explorer. Wegener was one of the first to combine the pre-historical with the historical in both time and space. He began to look for, and find, cases of similar fossil organisms separated by oceans. He particularly noticed the close fit between the coastlines of Africa and South America (Wegener 1915), which eventually earned him the appellation 'Father of Plate Tectonics.' As a geographer I had heard of Wegener, but had no idea how much of a presence he had established in Greenland, particularly in Uummannaq Fjord. Although not trained as an archaeologist, he practiced the same precision in the field as does an archaeologist. Wegener's *raison d'être* was to "reestablish the connection between geophysics on the one hand and geography and geology on the other, which had become completely ruptured because of the specialized development of these branches of science" (Wegener 1912). His theory of continental drift has become his foremost contribution to geophysical science.

## Greenland Expeditions: 1929–1931

Over a period of 24 years, Wegener was a member of four Greenland expeditions. The first two expeditions, to east Greenland, preceded World War I. After the war, the next two expeditions were to west Greenland with its longer season of ice-free days. The North Atlantic Drift, an extension of the Gulf Stream, warms the waters of west Greenland while northern polar waters, which flow from Siberia, cool the waters of east Greenland. Both of the west Greenland expeditions were to the Uummannaq/Disko Bay region. The first, the 1929 *Vorexpedition*, was essentially a reconnaissance mission to locate the most favorable access point to the Greenland Ice Cap. The route Wegener chose was through Uummannaq Fjord, the world's second largest fjord. One objective was to locate a glacier that would connect "…directly to the Inland Ice [Greenland Ice Cap] which did not calve icebergs directly into the sea. The connection to the ice cap by way of a coastal glacier indicated that the 'West Station' need not be 100 kilometers or more inland; it could be there on the coast. This would be an enormous saving of time and energy" (Greene 2015, 567). Ascent of that route proved to be more difficult than Wegener envisioned.

Wegener's boat the Krabbe,
anchored in Uummannaq,
in the foreground of the two
peaks of Uummannaq's
namesake mountain
*The camera angle places
the mast between the two peaks.
Trips between Ukkusissat
and Uummannaq, about 10km
(6mi) were made to return
workers and dogs home and to
pick up supplies. Compare
this image with the built—up
landscape of the book cover.
Image from Knudsen-
Holm family archives used
with permission.*

## Settlement of Ukkusissat

*North of Uummannaq on fjord's northern edge, this settlement provided both dogs and workers for Wegener's West Station. In the background is what has become known as Alfred Wegener Peninsula. Further up the waterway behind Ukkusissat, on the vertical face of that Peninsula, is the Black Angel Mine. The settlement provided workers for the Black Angel Mine until it closed.*

*left to right:*

### Wegener navigates through ice pack

*Gabrielsen (on the right) was one of best dog sledge drivers in Greenland. He was also an excellent machinist, familiar with the type of engine on the Krabbé, and was the "ship husband", or general minder of the boat. He taught Wagener's European crew how to drive a dog team. Before Wegener, Gabrielsen was an expedition companion of Knud Rasmussen. In 1916/1917, he served with Rasmussen on the Second Thule Expedition, exploring and charting Melville Bay and the coast of northern Greenland (Greene 2015, 566; Brown 2015, 159-160). Image from Knudsen-Holm family archives used with permission.*

### Alfred Wegener and Tobias Gabrielsen

*Riding on bowsprit of the Krabbe, Wegener makes one of his many trips, ferrying men, dogs, or supplies between Kamarajuk and Uummannaq. Image from Knudsen-Holm family archives used with permission.*

In Greenland, Wegener, already famous as a climatologist and meteorologist, became a friend of Northern District Manager Aage Knudsen in Jakobshavn, now Ilulissat. During the second and main expedition, from 1930 to 1931, Wegener established two sites: West Station above Uummannaq Fjord and Mid-Ice Station (*Eismitte*) about 400km (250mi) inland on the ice cap. These two sites would be part of a system of three climatological stations; the third, East Station at Scoresbysund in east Greenland, was established at the same time.

The expedition had three primary objectives. First, the thickness of the ice cap would be measured using seismic techniques, i.e., explosions in ice accompanied by the measurement of sound reflections with a seismometer; second, the elevation of the ice cap relative to sea level would be profiled. Third, and perhaps most important, to measure the effect of Greenland on weather, three weather stations would be arrayed along a line at 71° north latitude.

## West Station to Mid-Ice Station, *Eismitte*

The location of West Station was based on advice solicited from the local populace, and on extensive cruises on the 10m (30ft) locally built expedition boat *Krabbe*. Uummannaq, a second port for *Krabbe*, served as a base for Wegener's boat during much of the expedition, ferrying supplies, dogs and personnel between the expedition base on the north side of Uummannaq Fjord, near the settlements of Ukkusigssat on Kamarajuk Fjord, with Uummannaq Island on the south side of Uummannaq. A black and white image shows Wegener and Tobias Gabrielsen, Wegener's able Greenlandic authority on travel in Greenland by both land and sea.

**Iceberg serves as frame**
*Near Ukkusissat we motored around this iceberg, artistically carved by nature, that framed a long-abandoned shelter.*

While on a trip in 2010 to visit Illorsuit, where American artist Rockwell Kent lived and painted in the 1930s, our party from Uummannaq, traveling in three open boats, made a stop at Ukkusigssat. Color images taken on this trip in 2010 show the location of Ukkusigssat at the tip of the peninsula. Beyond is the channel that leads to where the West Station had once been. On the preceding page, an image of an iceberg frames a weather-beaten wooden shelter that stands on the shore.

Our plan had been to turn inland, then north and east, towards the Black Angel Mine (see Chapter 2). However, the wind was so strong that our boats could have easily blown over. As there was a recent incident of such a catastrophe, we changed course to Ilorsuit. Hurricane-like winds reminded me of the katabatic winds which flow from the heights of Antarctica to the sea. I did not know at the time that Ukkusissat region was a location Wegener had explored, and also where he died, in 1930. The Black Angel Mine (lead and zinc, some silver) is actually located south of Kamarutjuk (or Black Bight) Fjord near the entrance to a small fjord. The mine is on the east side of the fjord while the processing facility is on the west side. An aerial tramway crosses the fjord, connecting the mine at an elevation of 700m (2,300ft) with the processing plant at sea level (Map 4).

*left to right:*
**Sledge with metal runners being used as an external pack frame**
*This was back in the days before Kelty, North Face, Dana Design, and REI—even before the famous Appalachian pack boards. Image from Knudsen-Holm family archives used with permission.*
**Kamarutjuk (Black Bight) Fjord and Krabbe**
*A landing point at the base of the fjord offered protection for the removal of tons of equipment, supplies, expedition members, and dogs. Kamarutjuk was the starting point for the ascent of Kamarutjuk Glacier on to Scheideck, and what was to become West Station. Image from Knudsen-Holm family archives used with permission.*

Kamarutjuk Fjord, about 10km (6mi) north of Uummannaq Island on the north side of Uummannaq Fjord, nestled among peninsulas behind the settlement of Ukkusissat, was the primary expedition port for West Station and Scheideck (the Divide). With the closing of the Black Angel Mine (Mármorilik) in 1990, Ukkusissat, a small village to begin with, lost much of its population. The village now relies mostly on fishing for support. Kamarutjuk Fjord, with its glacier, was essentially the beginning of the land route to West Station, Scheideck, and then on to Mid-Ice Station.

While on the Greenland Ice Cap, Wegener maintained contact with Aage Knudsen. Wegener's messages detailed the hardships encountered in that season's inland passage. (Also see 'Dedication to Inger Knudsen Holm Morse'). Later, Aage's daughter Inger translated those messages into English, and she shared them with me at her home in Owls Head, Maine. In his last written message from the ice, Wegener wrote that travel conditions were extremely difficult: too much ice on the sea and too much snow on the inland ice.

In Uummannaq Fjord, the Wegener party had looked for a glacier that was not too fast flowing, not too steep to minimize crevasses, and with the snout of the glacier not too far removed from the coast to minimize boulder fields and the deep mud of glacial till deposits. "The most appropriate glacier

**Glacial stream crossing**
*Before any elevation can be gained, a confusion of braided melt-water streams must be crossed. Image from Knudsen-Holm family archives used with permission.*

turned out to be the Kamarutjuk Glacier, which flowed in a southwesterly direction towards the sea....Access to the inland ice had been found." (Diemberger 2015 [1999], no pagination)

For the Wegener expedition, backpacking tons of equipment from Ukkusigssat to Kamarajuk Glacier, a distance of 26km (16mi) was a tortuous, physical challenge. To ascend to the Greenland Ice Cap was not a straightforward hike up a gently sloping glacier. Rather, myriad natural obstacles were encountered: stream crossings, house-size boulders, loosely consolidated moraines, hidden ice crevasses, and ice falls. In this, its first phase, the expedition ascended 915m (3,000ft) up Kamarajuk Glacier to Scheideck and West Ice Station (McCoy 2006, 77). More often than not, neither dogs nor propeller-driven sleds (a new, yet unproven, technology) were up to the task. Base camp was established on a *nunatak* (a mountain peak protruding though land ice) at an elevation of 975m (3,199ft) and named 'Scheideck', located between the Kamarajuk and Kangerdluarsuk Glaciers (Motte 2015, 568). There, perhaps, little time for relaxation could be found. Finally, sufficient preparatory field logistics had been accomplished to have time for science, when Wegener could drill ice core samples or perhaps drill a hole in the ice to insert dynamite and seismically measure ice thickness. In Seismology, sound waves from an explosion are analyzed to gauge thickness of the ice and to profile the underlying rock. Field preliminaries to ensure survival and some level of comfort in the Arctic determine how much science can be conducted.

West Station was established above Kamarutjuk Fjord near Scheideck. The Mid-Ice Station was also established at a midpoint on the Greenland Ice Cap. A three-prong strategy was involved, much of which consisted of activity that rapidly drew down the limited resources of men and equipment.

## Wegener and party trekked inland to set up base camp on Ice Sheet

*Although a convenient glacier was located by which to access the polar ice cap, images made by the Wegener team show that this access point led the party through a gauntlet of obstacles, including a heavily bouldered washout plain, glacial melt streams, icefalls, and steep moraines with loose sand, gravel, and rocks. The party finally reached the glacier itself, with its oft hidden crevasses. Loads that had to be carried were not designed with backpacking in mind. Notes sent by Alfred Wegener to Aage Knudsen in Jakobshavn and later translated into English by daughter Inger Knudsen, detail the exhausting travel conditions marked by dangerous crevasses, little snow, and steep inclines— often beyond the ability of dogs and mechanized snow machines to ascend. Images from Knudsen-Holm family archives used with permission.*

*left to right:*

**Wegener and Villumsen**

*Wegener and Rasmus Villumsen engage in conversation. It was Villumsen who was to accompany Wegener from Mid-Ice Station on the trek back to West Station. Wegener died from a heart attack on the expedition. Villumsen continued on but also died at some unknown place on the ice. Images from Knudsen-Holm family archives used with permission.*

**Wegener drills an ice core sample**

*Upon reaching the Inland Ice (Greenland Ice Cap), ice coring begins with which to profile ice age, thickness, and composition. Image from Knudsen-Holm family archives used with permission.*

The first task was to build and maintain West-Ice Station. Almost concurrently, the Mid-Ice Station would be constructed and maintained. To build and maintain these two stations required transportation linkages needed to ferry tons of equipment and supplies a distance of 400km (250mi), through an elevation change of about 1000m (3000ft), to a final elevation of about 3,000m (9,000ft) at a point on the Greenland Ice Cap midway between Uummannaq and Scoresbysund.

With winter ever closer and with Mid-Ice Station still short of supplies and equipment, even after three round-trip supply runs, each of 800km (500mi), Wegner decided that a fourth supply run was needed. Wegener personally led that supply mission, leaving West Station on September 2 and arriving at Mid-Ice Station seven weeks later on October 29. On November 1, at Mid-Ice Station, Wegener celebrated his 50th birthday. That same day, he left with Greenlander Rasmus Villumsen for the return trip to West Station with two sledges, one of which they had to abandon after traveling 254km (158mi) (McCoy 2006, 92). Wegener then turned to skis, still at high elevation, breathing air at -50° Celsius (-58° Fahrenheit). Later in November—estimates vary as to date—at 189km (118mi) from West Station, Wegener died of a massive heart attack.

Across the breadth of Greenland, all three stations had been successfully established, producing a yearlong climatological transect from Uummannaq to Scoresbysund. In 1932, by design, this climatology system that spanned the width of Greenland was deactivated.

Like Ernest Shackelton before him, who was laid to rest where he had once sought refuge on South Georgia Island, Wagener's interment was on the northern edge of Uummannaq Fjord. Later, the respective governments of England and Germany offered transportation back to their homeland for burial of their explorers, but their wives declined. Instead, the two men were laid to rest in those high latitudes where they literally 'spent' their lives: Shackelton was laid to rest on South Georgia Island; Wagener on " ...the peninsula in Greenland just to the north of Kamarajuk Glacier, now the Alfred Wegner Halvø (Peninsula), 71.10 north, 51.80 west (Motte 2015, 596).

Later, questions were raised about the cause of Wegener's death:

> ...Wegener's death was blamed on a chain of unfortunate accidents, especially bad weather conditions. Using material that was hidden in the archives, this paper examines several additional aspects of the story, such as the influence of the Notgemeinschaft der Deutschen Wissenschaft (Emergency Society for German Science), which financed the expedition; and concludes that the erroneous judgments of individuals can be blamed for Wegener's death... (Lüdecke April 2000)

The literature is not clear on the factors that led up to Wegener's death. Would an inland trek from east Greenland to west Greenland have been preferable? The Uummannaq route did not possess as many advantages as envisioned. There was too much equipment and supplies that had to be manhandled, some of it needlessly, to Mid-Ice station. There were equipment issues: the two propeller-driven motor sleds that were to be central to logistics proved worthless. Communication between West Station and Mid-Ice Station, as well as with sleds en route, was nonexistent. Although two-way radios were available, the decision was made that they may not perform and that they were too bulky. Air support, also then available, was ruled out. In addition, there were a few personality differences to compound the hardships (Greene 2015, 539, 597; McCoy 2006 Chapter 11).

Wegener was in every sense a 'polymath' of the earth sciences. Like Knud Rasmussen, Therkel Mathiassen, and Frederica de Laguna, Wegener was both scientist and pioneer. While not recognized as scientists, contemporary early 20th century explorers who were innovators in the Arctic include Peter Freuchen, Frederick Cook, Robert Peary, Donald MacMillan, and Bob Bartlett. Intellectually and spiritually, they all engaged the challenges faced for survival in the Arctic.

**Atitsiak**
*Polar Bear Standing by Elias Semigak (Inuit). Nain, Labrador. Carved from green virginite, found on Newfoundland's Baie Verte Peninsula. 2013. 8" high.*

# 7

# Climate Change

Homo sapiens won the grand lottery of evolution...a
gargantuan power to extract the nonrenewable resources of
the planet....[T]he evolutionary innovations that made
us dominant over the rest of life also left us sensory cripples.
It rendered us largely unaware of almost all the life in
the biosphere that we have been so heedlessly destroying.

*Edward O. Wilson. The Meaning of Human Existence. (2014, 80, 90).*

But the question of what constitutes dangerous climate
change raises another question—dangerous to whom?
For the Inuit, whose primary food resources of caribou and
seal are now difficult to find as a result of climate change,
an economically and culturally dangerous threshold has
been crossed.

*Tim Flannery. The Weather Makers. (2005, 169).*

The collective activity of humanity is sapping the ecological
basis of civilization.

*Benjamin Kunkel .London Review of Books. (2017 March 2, 22).*

E. O. Wilson muses about our microscopic, just discernible wispy blue planet as it travels like a space ship through the unknowable vastness of the Milky Way Galaxy, and all that we have is what is on that space ship *Earth*. NASA photos of Earth, seen through the strikingly dramatic rings of Saturn, from the Cassini satellite, in 2013, show how starkly alone 7.3 billion of us are on our space ship, a dot in a sea of apparent nothingness. Meanwhile, we, as the winners in evolutionary selection, are fouling our planetary home.

Climate change is an important part of the Uummannaq story. Hunters claim that the most important consequence of climate change is not warmer temperatures *per se*; but the increasingly erratic nature of the weather. Like the polar bear that reads all the fluctuations in the Arctic weather, humans hunting in the Arctic are also guided by a cumulative knowledge of weather patterns passed down through the generations; patterns that reveal the 'when', 'where', what', and 'how' to track prey. This knowledge is the essence of survival. I learned this well once, on the ice of Baffin Bay, off Bylot Island in northern Nunavut, because I did not know how to read the ice. Moving across darker ice with the texture and stability of slush, I began to sink. Upon close look and touch, one sees that dark ice is spring ice filled with swirling clouds of phytoplankton and zooplankton. Dark ice is honeycombed, and supports little weight. Fortunately, I rolled my upper body onto denser, whiter ice and then dragged myself (with some assistance) onto the hard blue ice. Knowledge and experience go hand-in-hand. Climate change increases the risk of travel on Arctic ice as well as on icy American and European highways.

Lisa Mastny, editor of World Watch's annual environmental report, *State of the World*, writes:

> *The Inuit lay claim to an ethic they call Akisussaassuseq, a sense of responsibility toward the land, the water, and all the creatures that live there. The Inuit had achieved an environmentally sustainable society thousands of years ago—they had little choice but to do so. Today, of course, they can choose just like the rest of us. Choice—in all sorts of bewildering forms—is a sort of shockwave effect of the collision with mainstream culture. (World Watch Magazine, January/February 2000)*

Writer and frequent Arctic visitor Elizabeth Kolbert writes of an Inuit hunter John Keogak on the Inuit Canadian side of Baffin Bay who speaks of the diminishment of Arctic culture through global warming as harbinger for all cultures:

> *It's not just happening in the Arctic. It's going to happen all over the world. The whole world is going too fast. (Kolbert 2007, 5)*

Ironically, climate change has become a primary reason for tourists to visit Greenland. The support infrastructure developed by largely local interests in response has transformed a subsistence culture into that of a western market culture.

Nevertheless, this generalization is more pertinent to the market economy of Ilulissat than to the more traditional economy of Uummannaq. The economy of Ilulissat is characterized by a well-developed aggregation of tourist facilities, including airlines, four-star hotels, Arctic craft shops, a substantial marina, and an array of restaurants. By contrast, the economy of Uummannaq continues largely within the tradition of extractive hunting and fishing, although fishing has become a market-oriented element of the economy; hunting much less so.

With the diminishing role of the hunter as the model upon which Greenlandic social structure is founded, a problem arises when young men are separated from the traditional role of man as hunter. One consequence of this cultural disconnect is that many young people fall under dire circumstances and, of necessity, become wards of the state. This is where a children's home, such as Børnehjemmet in Uummannaq, comes into play. There are implications for the current as well as for succeeding generations.

Climate change has wrought significant far-reaching changes to the education curriculum. While the mission statement of Børnehjemmet emphasizes traditional ways of hunting and fishing—the traditional basis of Arctic survival skills—as the primary means for individual develop-ment, the school curriculum has been enhanced to include a number of marketable skills that address the potential consequences of climate change. While students continue to learn how to live off the land from aging elders, and practice traditional skills associated with the arts, clothing, shelter, and hunting and fishing, their teachers also emphasize computer skills and introduce them to such areas as western music, arts, and crafts; retailing; and the techniques of building construction. In addition, students learn to read and converse in the Greenlandic, Danish, and English languages, which is required in order to qualify for university enrollment in Denmark.

Environmental education at the Children's Home encourages a respect for and care of the environment. The basic precepts are:

- Humans should not exceed the ability of nature to replace what is taken.
- The environment should not be polluted.
- The conservation ethic applies to all uses of energy and resources.

With climate change, the temperature of Arctic waters has increased and the season for dog sledging has been shortened considerably from its usual months of December into June. In the winter of 2013/2014, dog sledging could not begin until February. In recent years, the sledging season has generally lasted only about six weeks, rather than its traditional six-to-seven months. Sufficient sea ice that is thick and extensive enough to permit safe travel has been lacking in Uummannaq for much of the last decade.

As a consequence, dogs are no longer accustomed to hunting. In the old days of seal hunting, dogs would remain quietly in place as instructed; now they howl and fight and are generally undisciplined. Increasingly, it is seen as much easier to use snow machines than it is dogs, for sledging. Yet the rules of the Government of Greenland limit use of the snow machine only to bring fish from the ice to the plant for processing. Nevertheless, the local community has interpreted the rule liberally, in hunting as well as fishing. The expanded application of the rule has gone unnoticed.

With warming temperatures, the most important factor that affects seal hunting is the reduction of fast ice, i.e., the seasonal formation in the Uummannaq Fjord of local ice that is connected to land. The absence of fast ice requires the hunter to travel by boat to shoot a swimming, dark-colored seal in black rolling water from a pitching deck. This is much more of a challenge than is hunting a sunbathing seal on white ice, shooting from the stability of a prone position. With fewer seals killed, the Greenlandic dietary demand for protein and fat can only be marginally satisfied through the purchase of expensive, imported, meats at the Pilersuisoq outlet.

Climate change has attracted a number of travelers with an interest in the environment to Uummannaq to observe the melting process. The three stories below highlight the alarmingly rapid shrinkage of Arctic ice—both the millennially aged Greenland icebergs from the Greenland Arctic Ice Cap and the annually formed fast ice. As a common point of reference, each of these three cases constitutes a creative endeavor to raise political awareness regarding the dramatic and harmful impact of global warming on the Arctic climate, indigenous cultures, and wildlife.

## Cool(e)motion—Nature as Art

Beginning at least 36,000 years ago, as exemplified by the Chauvet Cave paintings of southern France, our ancestors used art to record the human relationship with nature. Today, Dutch artist Ap Verheggen expresses nature as art within the context of climate and culture. Verheggen maintains that climate change has always been with us, and in that sense, climate change has always changed human culture. Through sculptures such as 'Cool(e) motion', Verheggen uses art to dramatize the effect of climate change on the environment. The parallel role of science, he maintains, is to find the truth, i.e., the causes of climate change and how to constructively respond.

from top:
**A last visit**
*Three days after this photo was taken, Cool(e)motion broke up, and the sculpture sank to the depths of the fjord.*
**Cool(e)motion 'sets sail'**
*A lot of energy and resources, both artistic and physical, were invested in this politically motivated project.*

Verheggen's sculpture consisted of two dog sledges crafted from heavy, flexible cable. On March 22, 2010, a helicopter lifted the sledges onto a drifting iceberg. This composition, representing nature as art or art as nature, placed climate change on a human scale to raise consciousness of climate change. Humans may put the sculpture of a dog sledge on an iceberg, but afterwards, nature is in charge as the sculpture drifts until the iceberg breaks up and dissolves into the sea, raising public awareness of global warming. Through an arrangement with Google Earth, GPS units were placed on the sculpture, to track the iceberg as it coasted with the natural forces of water and wind. As a strategic element of the project's artistry, Verheggen made provision for viewers from around the planet to comment on climate change from their place on the planet in a system similar to sticking 'post-its' on a bulletin board. The intent was to create a worldwide citizen-based statement on climate change that could then be used to leverage political power to address the issue.

Traveling by boat, we tracked the iceberg in seven closely-spaced field trips between May 18 and May 30, 2010. On our last visit, one of the crew, Jens, a neurosurgeon from Switzerland, climbed on the iceberg and walked nearly 75m (250ft) along the surface towards the sculpture. Then, sensing that this mature ice mass could turn over or break apart at any time, without warning, Jens quickly began his descent (compare the closeness of the sculpture to water in the images. With Jens safely back on board, we paid our last homage with a group cheer to Verheggen's creation. Three days later, on May 30, the iceberg disintegrated and the sculpture sank into the dark icy waters of Uummannaq Fjord. Nature prevailed but in the process short-changed the artist's political message.

## Showtime Television—Discovery of the North

A few years later, in 2013, Lesley Stahl, a well-known host with an American television news feature program and several of her colleagues, came to Uummannaq to produce reports both on Greenland Day and on climate change in the Arctic. Metaphorically, much of the western media views Green-land as the 'big gun' with which to deliver the message of climate change as

*clockwise from top right:*
**'60 Minutes' film crew**
*In June, 2013, filming began for a US Showtime Television feature on 'Greenland Day'.*
**Dinner with Ann and the '60 Minutes' crew**
*Leslie Stahl and production crew, and the rest of us in the photograph, exchanged stories of how we all came to be at Ann's dinner table in Greenland.*
**Uummannaq heliport**
*The crew continues shooting as Leslie Stahl and the Air Greenland pilot discuss details of flight to ice fields above Ilulissat.*

established fact. At dinner in Ann's house with Stahl and the
film crew, we each told our story of the path that brought us to Greenland.
Later, Ms. Stahl and the production crew flew by helicopter to the
Greenland ice sheet and the glaciers behind Ilulissat. Before the crew left
for Ilulissat, preparations were made at the heliport for more filming.

## Nuussuaq Peninsula by Air

Images of the Nuussuaq Peninsula have been gathered in three ways.
First, they were gathered during the trek over the peninsula with children
from the Children's Home (this trek along the International Appalachian
Trail was discussed above, in Chapter 5: Current Economy). The second was
travel by boat along the south shore of Nuussuaq Peninsula, where a truly
dramatic recession of the glaciers is seen. As glaciers melt they leave behind
a moraine of rock, sand, and clay that the glaciers have scoured, transported,
and deposited, on land and in the sea. Glacial remnants float out to sea in an
iceberg, and as the iceberg melts rock and other sediment are deposited on
the sea floor.

*from left:*
**Glacial recession on Nuussuaq Peninsula**
*These images illustrate pilot Jens Larsen's comment
about this peninsula as "a case study of climate change."
The image on the left is an excellent record of ice pack,
which has receded upwards to colder elevations. The
image above portrays a previously glaciated landscape
that, through glacial recession, is rapidly advancing to
desert-like desiccation.*
**Image presents an eroded, scared land characterized
by carved rock and moraines of scoured rock material**
*As glacial ice melts, a trail of detritus, which is of interest
to climate scientists, advances towards the sea. Geological
studies track sediment composition and characterize the
distribution of sediment on the floor of the North Atlantic
Ocean. This section of Greenland is increasingly resembling a similarly colored region of the US, Arizona.*

**Glacial moraines**
*Formation of new ice cannot compensate for the rate of ice mass loss, which leads to retreat of the terminus of the glacier. Without ice, this Arctic landscape could be New Mexico or Arizona.*

The third source is images taken from the air during the course of several flights with Air Greenland, by helicopter, and with Airzafari in a small fixed wing aircraft. Aerial observation from small aircraft presents the most dramatic view of glacier recession and the dramatic proliferation of icebergs. One flight, from Qaarsut to Ilulissat in an Air Greenland DASH-7, carried only a few passengers. Ellen Christoffersen asked if I would like to fly in the jump seat up front with the pilots. "Of course!" Air Greenland pilot Jens Larsen was glad for my company and I enjoyed an extended tour of the Nuussuaq Peninsula on the way back to Ilulissat. The recession of the Nuussuaq ice cap was striking. Previously, the glacier terminated at the sea's edge but now it terminates before reaching the sea. Now, icebergs cannot calve into the sea as the face of the glacier is somewhat inland, and water from melted ice carrying sediment flows across land before discharging into the sea. Much of that landscape, one can say, now resembles the predominately dry peaks of the American southwest, which are located at considerably lower latitude. Jens commented that glacial disappearance on Nuussuaq is a case study of climate change, a dramatic situation that is the purpose of his tours.

The view from the jump seat of the DASH-7 as we approached the Ilulissat airstrip, was a panorama of ice. From the ground, and from the Arctic Hotel, which overlooks the sea from a butte, the vista was almost that of a blockade created from ice calved from the Jakobshavn Isbrae (glacier). Larson and his wife Bente own Airzafari, a three plane touring company. Through Airzafari flights, Jens and Bente raise consciousness of the frightening rate of loss of ice in Greenland by focusing on the rapidly shrinking ice sheet that has dominated the mountainous spine of Nuussuaq Peninsula.

*clockwise from top left:*

**Iceberg bigger than town of Ilulissat**

*This iceberg, which has drifted towards Ilulissat, is larger than the town itself. In this image, the town is nestled just above the iceberg. Beyond the town is the Ilulissat airport.*

**Pilots and husband and wife team Jens Ploug Larsen and Bente Biilmann Larsen**

*Bente obtained her pilot's license in Texas. Many pilots who fly for Air Greenland or other companies in Greenland have done their pilot training in Texas and retain certification through regular re-training in Texas.*

**Icebergs from Jakobshavn Isbrae (Glacier)**

*From the sky over the ice-choked waters of Ilulissat, Jakobshavn ice, flowing from the Greenland Ice Sheet, can be visually tracked to Greenland's horizon.*

**Icebergs in Jakobshavn Ice Fjord**
*Discharged ice builds up at a choke point at the entrance to Ilulissat's harbor before it is released into the waters of Disko Bay.*

**Aerials of East Greenland**

*For purposes of comparison, the mountain peaks of east Greenland just barely protrude through ice and glaciers. Siberian waters bring cold water south to east Greenland. By comparison, North Atlantic Drift brings warm water north to west Greenland. Sea currents definitely affect ice conditions, both at sea and on land.*

Another of the regular Airzafari tours is of Jakobshavn Isbrae (glacier) and its iceberg congestion in Disko Bay. Airborne again, this flight brings the same icebergs into view from the side opposite the Arctic Hotel. Finally the Jakobshavn ice stream comes into view as it flows down from the two-mile high Greenland ice sheet, many miles away on the horizon, into the waters of Ilulissat and Disko Bay. On average, Jakobshavn Isbrae discharges 40 km$^3$ of ice per year. (Pelto 2008).

Cold water flowing out of the Arctic Ocean into the Greenland Sea controls ice melt on the east side of Greenland. By contrast, on the west side, the relatively warmer waters of the North Atlantic Drift, which is an offshoot of the Gulf Stream, increase the rate of ice melt. Ice melt on the east coast of Greenland is much less than on its west side.

## Ilulissat Climate Days and Jakobshavn Ice Fjord

In 2015 I was invited to attend the Ilulissat Climate Days conference. The National Science Foundation provided travel to Greenland aboard a U.S. Air Force C-130. Ilulissat Climate Days, which was sponsored by an impressive array of Arctic research institutions, brought together 158 Arctic specialists to share with one another their knowledge of climate change and ice conditions in the Arctic. The primary venue for the conference was Ilulissat's Hotel Arctic. Conference sponsors included the lead agency, Denmark's National Space Institute (DTU), as well as the Nordic Council of Ministers, the European Space Agency, the International Arctic Science Committee, the National Aeronautics and Space Administration, the National Science Foundation, the Geological Survey of Denmark and Greenland, the Hotel Arctic, and others. As a contributor to a poster session, I combined historical photos from the Knudsen-Holm collection with my own imagery to present a visual, century-long history of the Ilulissat (Jakobshavn)/Uummannaq region. In this fashion, two large collections of images, each collection covering the same Jakobshavn/Uummannaq region and with about a century in between, document change in people and place, making interesting comparisons possible.

At the Ilulissat Climate Days conference, many Arctic scientists presented field-based studies of Jakobshavn glacial melt. Stimulated by the conference, and only a few miles from Jakobshavn Glacier itself, I decided to see for myself after the conference. I remembered Jens Larsen and his charter service Airzafari. Although Jens was in Copenhagen, one of his pilots took me on a low-level flight of the Jakobshavn Glacier. In recent years, the glacial terminus where calving occurs in Jakobshavn has been moving inland approximately 600 meters—more than a third of a mile—each year. But, no matter how far inland that ice is calved, that ice eventually exits Greenland into Baffin Bay at an increasing rate.

One of the lead modelers is Konrad Steffen whose work is based on data from 25 automated weather stations he has installed in Greenland. Jason Box, of the Geological Survey of Denmark and Greenland (GEUS), reported on his modeling of ice sheet climatology and surface mass balance. A common objective in their studies was to understand the relationships that tie elevation, precipitation, and surface melting. Through its Climate Change Initiative (CCI), the European Space Agency (ESA) tracks changes in ice mass. The data show that there is more ice melt in Greenland than

*from top left:*
**Distant view looking towards Greenland Ice Sheet**
*Notice that this mass of ice is already fractured. Dirt exposed by the melting surface increases glacial melt rate well before reaching the sea and calving. Calving is popularly perceived as happening upon reaching the sea, not before.*
**Konrad Steffen**
*Director of the Swiss Federal Research Institute, Dr. Steffen is a leader in Arctic climate research. He spoke at the Ilulissat Climate Days Conference. June 2015.*
**Like water, ice eddies around a nunatak, a mountain protruding through the ice sheet**

in the Canadian territories of Ellesmere and Baffin combined. This phenomenon was particularly pronounced in 2010 and 2012. Several different models used the same data in different ways. All reveal the same trend in decreasing Greenland ice mass. In its climate change studies in Greenland, a Nordic research initiative called 'Stability and Variations of Arctic Land Ice' (SVALI), found, like GEUS, that there is loss of ice through melting at lower elevations of Greenland. However, the volume of ice at higher, central elevations continues to increase, because, as the atmosphere and oceans warm, evaporation and precipitation increase, causing increased snowfall at higher elevations in Greenland.

Jakobshavn Isbrae, or Jakobshavn Glacier, is not simply a well-known outlet glacier to the sea, rather—like a major waterway—it is the merging of a mass of meandering glaciers joined into an 'ice stream'. (It is only when a pilot flies at low altitude that an ice mass can be identified and classified as an 'ice stream'). Based on Antarctic research summarized by Graham (2011, 599) in the *Encyclopedia of Snow, Ice and Glaciers,*

**From my hotel window in Ilulissat**
*A mellow evening light conveys tranquility between the icebergs and a kayaker.*

*from bottom left:*
Like a river channel defined by topography, ice begins to channel into a major stream, the Jakobshavn Isbrae (Glacier).
A prominent ablation (fracturing) area calves a wall of ice.
A calved wall, resembling the one in the image to the left, floats in Ilulissat waters.

*These streams represent the transition from interior flow to marginal or ice-shelf spreading, and serve to focus ice drainage (as well as water and sediment drainage) toward the coasts or ice sheet periphery, acting as large conveyor belts that deliver ice from centers of accumulation to areas of loss…. These ice streams originate from the ice sheet cores, and gradually increase in velocity downstream along their length… [they] have been described as the arteries of an ice sheet.*

Jakobshavn Ice Stream above, bends around a nunatak (a vertical rock obstruction around which the ice flows), flowing in a predominate pattern from east to west. Images sequentially track ice flow from the height of the Greenland Ice Sheet though its flow to the sea.

Research based on the modeling of environmental change in Greenland was an important component of Ilulissat Climate Days. This modeling effectively demonstrates the complexity of climate science as well as the worldwide impacts of climate change. Many factors were discussed that contribute to glacial ice melt in Greenland. By far, however, the most significant driver of glacial ice melt is the warming temperature of North Atlantic waters. Important findings presented at the conference, as summarized in (Richard and Willis, October 2015), include:

- The change in mass of the Greenland ice sheet can be measured by using 'space borne gravimetry'. As they pass overhead, a pair of orbiting satellites measure the gravitational attraction of the ice sheet. Changes in the gravitational field reflect changes in the mass of the ice. The data show that the amount of ice lost as the ice sheet melts and as icebergs break off the edge of the ice sheet is not compensated for by new snow and ice.

- Ice dynamics are a function of velocity (which is a function of the steepness of the outlet glacier), calving rate (which is related to ocean temperature) and sub-glacial hydrology (that is, dynamics of water acting in conjunction with ice, e.g., through calving of ice). Ultimately, it is the force of gravity that drives ice flow. Melting attributed to climate change can modify the frictional forces that resist ice flow. In this case, melt water that makes its way to the base of the ice sheet reduces friction between the ice mass and the underlying substrate, allowing faster flow. As the ocean becomes warmer, there is more evaporation and precipitation. Much of this precipitation falls as snow at higher elevations in central Greenland, which rise to over 3,000m (10,000ft). The increase in snowfall in central Greenland that can be attributed to increased evaporation from the sea does not compensate for the mass of ice lost at the edges and the mass balance difference (ice melt minus evaporation) contributes to an increase in sea level.

- The northern cryosphere is much further removed from the North Pole than is the southern cryosphere from the South Pole. The North Pole is not located on a land mass. It is located to the north of the North American Continent, under the Arctic Ocean. The South Pole is located on the continent of Antarctica where eons of geologic time provide for more expansive and deeper glaciation.

Another circumpolar feature distinguishes these two cryospheres from each other. Antarctica is endlessly circled by a continuous flow of salt water, which circumnavigates all 360° of Antarctica. Out at sea, this circling vortex of Antarctic Ocean water is contained within a perimeter of about 40° south latitude by the land abutments of the southern continents and by the denser composition of fresh water that is heavier than salt water.

Arctic Ocean temperatures of Greenland are influenced by the waters of Siberia drifting down along the north and east of that land mass. But, much of coastal Greenland has its temperatures moderated by warm North Atlantic Drift, which is spun into the waters of the North Atlantic from the Gulf Stream originating in the Gulf of Mexico.

In short, Arctic water ambient temperatures are likely to be warmer than are Antarctic waters. Proportional implications for warmer temperatures on Greenland means greater proportionate ice melt on both its land and water.

The American climatologist James Hansen reported findings that were very much in accord with those of Jason Box on the nonlinearity of ice melt and, for that matter, climate change. With 16 co-authors, Hansen recently wrote that he is reluctant to put any number on ice melt rates, which are proving to be "essentially an unpredictable, non-linear response of ice sheets to a steadily warming ocean". Using a combination of paleoclimate records, computer models, and observations, Hansen asserts that we are hurtling into uncharted waters. To quote from Hansen's abstract in Atmospheric Chemistry and Physics, "There is evidence of ice melt, sea level rise of 5m to 9m, and extreme storms in the [previous] interglacial period that was less than 10 Celsius warmer than today" (2015).

In his new book about climate transformation in the Arctic and its broader implications for the planet, Mark Serreze, Director of the U.S. National Snow and Data Center in Boulder, Colorado, writes:

> *The Arctic's soul is its cryosphere—its ice in all of its forms, which includes the floating sea-ice cover of the Arctic Ocean, snow, the Greenland ice sheet, ice caps, and glaciers (collectively glacial ice), ice on lakes and rivers, and permafrost. Whatever lives in the Arctic—be it flora or fauna—has adapted to coexist with the cryosphere. Serreze. Brave New Arctic (2018, 29)*

On the status of Greenland's ice mass:

> *…there is no doubt that the mass balance of Greenland [ice] has turned negative, meaning that the ice sheet is losing rather than gaining mass, and hence is contributing to sea-level rise….The recent mass losses for Greenland are larger than for the Antarctic ice sheet, and the mass loss from Greenland seems to have recently accelerated. (2018, 54)*

> *…over the period 1992 – 2011…both ice sheets had been loosing mass… with the largest contribution from Greenland. (2018, 201)*

On implication of Greenland's ice melting and rise in sea level:

> *The Greenland ice sheet is one of our planet's two ice sheets; the other is the Antarctic's ice sheet. The Greenland ice sheet [should it melt] …represents a little more than 7 meters [23 feet] of global sea level" throughout the planet's oceans. (2018, 143)*

William Nordhaus (2015, 37 – 38), too, writes about the unknowables, the increase in nonlinearities associated with climate change:

> *...[that] the standard analyses of climate change ignore our deep uncertainties about the extent and impacts of changes. They argue that recent developments in earth sciences and other studies suggest that the potential impacts of extreme events—what are known as "tail events" or sometimes more vividly as "black swans"—may dwarf the standard impacts described in the IPCC reports.*

Research published by Serreze supports this contention:

> *"The Greenland ice cap, for example, contains enough water, were it to melt, it would represent more than 7 meters (22.965') of global sea level." (2018, 143)*

At the end of December 2015, air temperatures over the Arctic briefly reached above freezing. Serreze, seemingly in disbelief, describes the event as:

> *"simply unheard of....The 2018 heat wave was the most extreme, with a temperature of 43° Fahrenheit recorded at Greenland's northernmost observatory, which is just 440 miles from the North Pole. For ten consecutive days, the station recorded above freezing temperatures." (2018, 60)*

These extreme events are buried in small numbers in the tails of a bell-shaped curve Although small in number, their impact is disproportionate. As an analogy, consider that the temperature of a healthy person measured over time averages 98.6° Fahrenheit. However, if for just one day the individual's temperature should rise to 105° Fahrenheit, mortality is certain and morbidity is possible.

Ethicist and environmental philosopher Dale Jamieson writes of the dramatic climate change that is apparently underway, as indicated by the decrease in width and depth of Arctic sea ice:

> *...Since modern measurements began, and perhaps much more if anecdotal and anthropological reports are to be believed....warming in the Arctic is much more extreme than in the mid-latitudes...with some Arctic regions having warmed 10 times as much as the mid-latitude average.... (2014, 213, 214).*

For two decades I have traveled in the arctic and subarctic regions of Greenland as well as in Nunavut, Labrador, and Québec's Lower North Shore in Canada. To a lesser extent I have also traveled Antarctic lands and waters. The magnitude of the Arctic's continent-sized cryosphere, of its breadth from Russia to North America, and of its thickness of 3.2km (2.0mi) on Greenland is difficult to comprehend. The reduction in size of this ice mass due to melting holds sobering implications for the weather of our biosphere and for most, if not all, of its life forms.

I am saddened and frustrated by the deplorable environmental concern demonstrated by world leaders not only in government, but also in business, the media, and amongst academics, politicians, and the general public. The most outspoken assessments of climate change have come from the IPCC, the Intergovernmental Panel on Climate Change.

With the benefit of my observations as a geographer and a photographer, I can help sound the alarm of climate change and the frightening implications of climate change for those who live off the radar, in the remote north in particular. With the implications of climate change now well recognized and documented, it is time to think beyond geopolitical borders. Reaching a consensus now with almost 200 separate nation states, variously located on the development continuum, requires time and patience, and we are running out of the former and do not have much of the latter.

The environmental problems we face are not confined to political borders. One dramatic example is seen in mercury emissions from coal-fired power plants in China that are deposited in Arctic waters and absorbed into the food chain. Mercury is passed up the food chain, and bioaccumulates in successively greater concentration as it does so. The accumulated mercury becomes successively more toxic, to the point that marine organisms including finfish, shellfish, seal, and whale—all-important elements of the Arctic diet—become unsafe to eat. Another example of cross-border pollution is soot produced by forest fires and the burning of agricultural fields in temperate zones that is carried to the Arctic by the prevailing winds. A consequence of soot deposits is that the albedo, the reflectivity, of snow and ice is reduced which, in turn, enhances the melt rate of snow and ice in the extensive Arctic biome.

But most critical is the significant change in albedo as polar ice melts to water. The albedo of ice, at 0.8/0.9 (reflectivity of 80 to 90 percent) drops to 0.07 for water, or roughly one-twelfth the reflectivity of snow or ice. (Kolbert 2007, 200) Solar energy that is absorbed by water, that would otherwise be reflected by snow and ice, contributes directly to warming of the water.

Carbon dioxide produced by the burning of fossil fuels readily dissolves in and increases the acidity of seawater. According to the Smithsonian Institution's National Museum of Natural History, at least one-quarter of the carbon dioxide ($CO_2$) that is released by fossil fuels dissolves into the ocean. Since the beginning of the industrial era, the earth's oceans have become 30 percent more acidic—faster than any known change in ocean chemistry in the last 50 million years. Increased acidity has an important negative consequence for finfish and shellfish, particularly so for shellfish, for which the formation and maintenance of the exoskeleton, or shell, is greatly impaired by acidic seawater (https://ocean.si.edu/ocean acidification).

**Ice tupilaks**
*Like the traditional mythical creatures of Inuit witchcraft made from ivory, then bone, these creatures shaped by nature from ice appear as foreboding harbingers of climate change.*

Climate change as measured by temperature increase is occurring twice as fast in the Arctic as elsewhere on the planet. Greenland, as a case in point, is too much of a harbinger of dramatic environmental change to be ignored. Dale Jamieson writes:

> *The ultimate source of our environmental problems is our separation from nature. The solution is to see us as part of nature. From this perspective, nature is inside of us and we are part of nature. (2014, 192)*

With the rate of decay of glaciers and the increased rate of calving of icebergs, we are in a new epoch, the Anthropocene, or 'the age of man' with its now unfolding 'unintended consequences' (Kolbert 2014). The present is the first time in human history that humanity has changed the climate of planet Earth. On planet Earth, we exist in a closed but complex less-than-understood weather system.

In 2016, I had arranged a dog sledging trip with René on Greenland's ice. April was chosen for the trip, for its longer periods of daylight and because it was well before the May/June melt season. But, a little more than a week before my arrival, in mid-April, much warmer, rain sodden air had moved from the mid-Atlantic to southwestern Greenland, advancing the earliest recorded start of Greenland's ice melt, from May 5 to April 11. April conditions followed "on the warmest winter (January 1 – March 31) recorded for the Arctic. Early melt events are important as they lower the surface albedo (reflectivity) by increasing the snow grain size. A lower albedo allows for more absorption of the sun's energy, fostering more ice melt (Jason Box April 12, 2016; Brian Kahn April 12, 2016; National Snow and Ice Data Center April 21, 2016)". The meter high ice figures shown to the left remind me of Inuit *tupilaks*, here as 'avenging monsters' of climate change.

Greenland still represents man living as part of nature. We dwellers of the mid-latitudes who are the planetary humans most removed from nature, who are most responsible for climate change, must aspire to find our place in nature as exemplified by our Greenlandic friends.

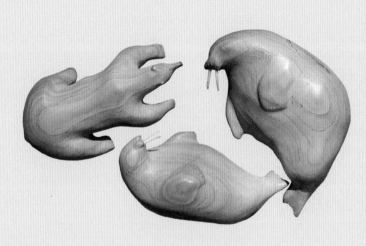

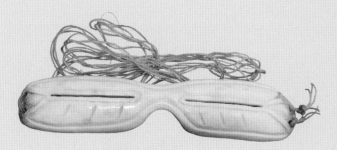

*left to right, from top left:*

**Fertile Woman**
*on Lanyard by Olive Binzer. Nuuk, Greenland. Narwhal. 2007. 3".*

**Kungutl \ Moon Mask**
*by Tim Alfred. Northwest Indian. Big Rapids, British Columbia. Face of mask is mother nature, herself. Moon beams are the four seasons of the year. The tufts on the outside of the moon represent the months of the year. 2008. 16".*

**Shaman's Flight**
*by Shawn Rumbolt (Metis). Moose antler and soapstone. St. Anthony, Newfoundland | Forteau, Labrador. 6" by 25". 2003.*

**"Ookpik", Arctic Snowy Owl**
*by John Terriak. Labradorite. Nain, Labrador. 2003. 5" high x 8" long.*

**Walruses and Polar Bear on Ice**
*by Ibey Kiyukikayuk. Arctic Bay, Baffin Island, Nunavut. 1982. Gray soapstone on reddish stone base. Base at 12" x 9" x height 3".*

**Black tupilak**
*Artist not known. Uummannaq, Greenland. 2015. 9" high x 3".*

**Muscular Polar Bear Walking**
*by Rachel Ootoova. Pond Inlet, Baffin Island, Nunavut. Marbled green soapstone. 2005. 12" long x 9" high.*

**Polar Bear Head Pendant**
*by Carl Petersen. Ilulissat, Greenland. Whale tooth. 2".*

**Inuit Face with Parka Hood**
*Unknown syllabic name. 2003. Bone. Grenfell Mission, St. Anthony, Newfoundland. 2" x 2".*

**Snow goggles**
*by Ross Kayotak. Caribou antler. Iqaluit, Nunavut, Canada. 5" width.*

**Dessicated Dwarf Willow**
*found while hiking Ellesmere Island in 2001. Less rain is received (2" annually) than in Sahara Desert. 7" high and 5" base*

# 8

# Culture

From... the wisdom of centuries, we know at last that
the universe does not revolve around us, that we are citizens
in a living community where our membership implies
stewardship, and that, contrary to Adam Smith's invisible
hand nonsense—those in pursuit of self bring suffering
to many.

*Carl Safina. The View from Lazy Point: A Natural Year in an Unnatural World (2011, 317).*

Indigenous culture in Greenland is a composite of values acquired
over a 4,500-year period, from Arctic Paleoeskimo to Thule cultures;
and from the technology of stone tools in a polar climate. These
cultures have subsequently been modified by nearly 500 years of a
competing western colonialism, giving birth to the culture known
as Greenlandic, which constitutes a comfortable and effective fit between
the Inuit communal model and the Scandinavian social model. This
melding of two congenial northern social systems is represented below in
the practice of communal and ecological values, as seen in arts and
crafts, music and dance, kayaking and dog sledging. Unlike most expressions
of European colonialism, particularly in the Arctic, Denmark has an established record of respect for Inuit culture.

*clockwise from top left:*
**Children's Art Program**
*Pierre Auzias teaches art to the children of Uummannaq. Here
are two life-size whimsical polar bears created by Pierre to
appeal to the town's children.*
**At the Smithsonian's Hirschhorn Museum and Sculpture Garden,
Washington, DC**
*Leaders and students of the Children's Home become as one
composition, framed by two rainbow colored triangles.*
**Culturally aware youth**
*Young Greenlanders take issue with an outside world that
condemns the killing of seals. The seal, which is used for food,
clothing, tools, and the skin of the kayak, is crucial to life in
Greenland.*

## Arts and Crafts

Through the guidance of French artist Pierre Auzias, residents of the
Children's Home create exhibits from discarded materials such as the card-
board tube from a roll of paper towel. Other materials that would otherwise
be discarded are used as art media. For example, a refrigerator door becomes
a canvas on which an Arctic seascape is painted. Travel to cities such as
New York, or Washington D.C., provides themes for artistic expression—
in this case—as paper mâché skyscrapers. These items are exhibited in
Uummannaq's Community Center as well as in Pierre's studio gallery
in Uummannaq and in the Children's Art Program.

**Uummannaq school concert**
*On-lookers at a concert show their appreciation, especially the four women—Heidi, Ann, Jonna, and Ellen.*

**Greenlandic polka**
*If Greenland had a national dance, it would have to be the polka, a dance for all ages.*

**If there is music in Uummannaq, Ron Alvarez is there**
*Here he conducts the school orchestra for children sitting up close on a bear skin rug, and later he plays with René and Svend.*

## Music and Dance

An array of resources may be found at the Children's Home itself, including guest artists from abroad who collaborate with the Uummannaq school system and cultural institutions such as Greenland's Katuaq Cultural Center in Nuuk. Music and dance performances—both traditional and modern— are a regular feature. Where else but above the Arctic Circle can one experience the music of a Greenlandic cellist, a Venezuelan violinist and conductor, an American from Vermont playing the Australian didgeridoo, a children's orchestra, and popular music—their singing accompanied by guitar, piano, and skin drums? The polka is a popular pastime in Uummannaq, including the Children's Home. As these images attest, Ron Alvarez, a composer and director from Venezuela, has built the musical program at the Children's Home into a much traveled, sought after orchestra.

In 2014, members of the Uummannaq Children's Orchestra traveled to Washington DC to perform at a program entitled Greenlandic Cultural Event held at the Smithsonian's Museum of Natural History. Composer Jean Michal La Vallee, who wrote the music for the film *Inuk*, conducted the Orchestra. In May 2015, Jean Michael and the Uummannaq Children's Orchestra returned to Washington for a performance at the Arctic Spring Festival, at which the United States assumed chairmanship of the Arctic Council. Other trips have included visits with Pete Seeger at his home in Beacon, New York. Until his passing in 2014, Seeger and Greenlanders were united in their music making.

**Kayak race held in commemoration of the 250th anniversary of founding of Uummannaq**
*A fleet of traditional Greenlandic kayaks circumnavigates Uummannaq Island. Fortunately, there was a relatively flat sea with little wind or ice.*

## Kayaking and Dog Sledging

### Kayaking

In the 1920's and 1930's, Greenlanders relied on the trademark sleek 'Greenland' kayak. In any Greenland village today, however, motorized boats are the basic means by which to extract a livelihood from the sea, as well as a way to just get about. Nevertheless, the sleek, pencil-like Greenland kayak is definitely making a cultural comeback, but not for any appreciable economic application except as a rental vessel for visitors or for traditional races. The Greenland kayak renaissance correlates with the popularity of kayaking, which began in North America in the 1970s. The traditional Arctic kayak, which is made from sealskin, can be a tasty treat for a dog, hungry-or-not. Throughout the settlements, sealskin kayaks are placed high on a rack or roof to keep them safe from the dogs.

### The original Greenland kayak

*A seal hunter silently strokes his sleek sea kayak forward, with hardly a ripple so that prey remain unaware. These handcrafted boats, made of sealskin and driftwood, are laden with appropriate technology developed for local conditions. Included are floats, an array of harpoons, and a patch of white canvas on the bow (qamutaasaq or taalutaq) to serve as camouflage while hunting. Image from Knudsen-Holm family archives used with permission.*

clockwise from top left:

**Maligiaq at Festival of Greenland**

*In 2005, Maligiaq built a kayak on the Mall in Washington D.C. He presented the kayak to the Smithsonian Institution, whose National Museum of Natural History sponsored the festival.*

**Arnie Nielsen and Lindsay**

*Posing with our new art work, the question was: How do we transport Arnie's heavy sculpture, chiseled from granite, home to Maine?*

**Maligiaq wins**

*There was little doubt that Maligiaq would finish first. Maligiaq, from the town of Sisimiut near Uummannaq, enjoyed well-deserved appreciation from the town of Uummannaq.*

As part of Uummannaq's 250th anniversary, a kayak race was held, in July 2013, that circumnavigated the island. Along with race officials and on-lookers in motorized vessels, about 30 kayaks assembled just outside Uummannaq's harbor. With sleek, traditional Greenlandic kayaks ready at the starting buoys, the race was underway at noon. Maligiaq, from Sisimiut, won the race with a time of 1 hour 41 minutes. Uummannaq's Arne Nielsen came in second, about one minute behind.

In 2005, Maligiaq visited the Smithsonian Institution in Washington, D.C. for the Festival of Greenland. While at the festival, Maligiaq crafted a kayak on the National Mall. After the festival, the kayak was donated to the Smithsonian and was exhibited in the Ocean Hall at the Smithsonian Museum of Natural History. Arne Nielsen is a stone carver who poses with Lindsay and his creation, *Many Faces*, in Uummannaq. Until May of 2018, that carving occupied a place on our back patio in Georgetown, Maine. Lindsay passed on May 24, 2018. Many Faces now resides above her grave in Georgetown's Mountainside Cemetery.

**Dog sledge finalists**
*With about 30 dog sledge teams competing in this annual Uummannaq spring race, these two teams led all other contenders.*

## Dog Sledging

The primary method of travel on ice in Greenland's Arctic remains the dog team, with at least six dogs pulling a sledge. In Greenland, the two most common forms of ice are 'fast ice' and 'glacial ice'. Fast ice freezes annually from the shore during the Arctic winter. Within fast ice, there is sub-classification: 'first-year ice', which builds up over a winter. Ice that builds up

*clockwise from top left:*
**Ole Møller attempts to feed his voracious dogs**
*Drop the food and get out of the way is the advice of those who know the dogs. Note that one airborne dog is only held to earth with a heavy chain.*
**Ludwig Hammeken feeds his sledge dogs**
*Apparently not as ravenous as Møller's dogs, Ludwig presents meat from a freshly killed seal.*
**Winner crosses the finish line**
*Even after the finish the dogs are still pulling strongly.*

**Providing for continuation of heritage**
*To encourage the next generation to drive dog teams, many of the racers will travel with one of their children aboard. Hunter Paulus Nikolajsen finished in fourth place with his son aboard.*

year-after-year is defined as 'multiyear ice'. With climate change, much ice—when there is ice—is simply first-year ice. 'Shore-fast ice' is fastened to land, giving quick, uninterrupted access from land to the sea. These 'ice highways' continue to experience shortened seasons. Yet, when there is ice, its safety is not assured. Without an 'ice highway,' hunting is reduced, as are visits among families and friends.

Glacial ice forms from snow on land, which through many years of accumulated snowfall, is compressed into ice. This ice then flows as a glacial river from the Greenland ice sheet to the sea, where icebergs calve and drift out to sea.

For much of the last decade climate change has adversely affected the formation of ice. With poor ice, or no ice, travel by dog sledge in Uummannaq Fjord has become very uncertain. As one result, travel by motorized boat is becoming the norm. But when there is ice, the sledges are brought out for hunting and fishing, and visiting friends and relatives. With ice, it becomes possible to hold the annual Uummannaq dog sledge race. A viewer sometimes sees an ice taxi out delivering friends and relatives for a visit. In Nunavut Territory in Canada, snow machines have largely replaced dog sledging. In Greenland, the use of snow machines has been discouraged by government policy, and it is not legal to use snow machines for either hunting or fishing. Ironically, the primary way that these machines are purchased is through income derived from fishing for halibut by dog sledge.

## *Inuk*—Film Premiere in Greenland

In May 2012, the official premiere of the Children's Home film *Inuk* was scheduled for release in Greenland, at that nation's Katuaq Cultural Center in Nuuk. The day before we were to leave Uummannaq for Nuuk, bad weather and a sick helicopter pilot resulted in cancelation of our flight from Uummannaq to Qaarsut, where we would pick up a fixed wing flight to Nuuk. The backup plan was to go to Qaarsut by snow machine. All eighteen of us in the party, as well as all our gear, had to be transported, but with thick fog and warm air, the ice was deteriorating rapidly.

**Field commander**
*Ann is a prime organizer: she knows what to do, how to do it, and when to do it.*

*from top:*
**Katuaq Cultural Center**
*Seats are filling up for the premier showing of Inuk in Greenland.*
**Rebekka, Albert, Unartoq, and Api await premier of the film**
*Since I know them well, they did not need to act, only to be themselves.*

Ann took charge, assembling our armada of snow machines and *komatiks* (sledges fitted with plywood boxes fitted on skis, pulled by a snow machine) to transport people and gear. One snow machine is needed to tow each komatik. By 6:00 AM, all of us were dressed in sealskin pants and polar bear anoraks and we were underway by 7:30 AM. The caravan snaked along the ice between pools of water, snowdrifts, and broken fast ice. At times we passed over ridges and slid down an incline onto the otherwise flat ice, all without benefit of any kind of suspension mechanism, experienced not as cushioned bumps but rather as abrupt, sudden crashes.

I rode up front with my computer, and Rebekka Jørgensen, who did the voice over in *Inuk*, rode with my camera bag. At many times visibility, while not a whiteout, was severely limited. At 8:30 AM, we approached Qaarsut, our destination. Since the ice was broken up into small flat fragments, we had to leave the komatik and walk, from ice cake to ice cake, to reach land. This experience makes me acutely aware of how isolated Uummannaq Island is without the helicopter.

Once we reached Qaarsut we learned that the fixed wing flight had been canceled. By 9:45 AM the runway was completely shrouded in fog—the other side of the runway was not visible. We spent the night in an airport hotel, which Air Greenland manages for weather-related events. Finally, on the following day, we left for Nuuk and a successful premier showing of *Inuk* at Katuaq.

**The actors and production company take repeated bows as the applause continues**
*With so much demand, a second showing was scheduled at Katuaq for the next day.*

Largely through the efforts of Børnehjemmet, townspeople, expatriates, and guests, Uummannaq exhibits a cornucopia of creative expression of both Western and Inuit origin. Guest musicians present Uummannaq's young people with a wide array of potential mentors. Meanwhile, skin boats, both the one-person kayak and the multi-person umiak (women's boat) are making a comeback, and are enjoyed by residents and visitors alike.

Greenlanders are thoughtful people, open to sharing and to new ways of doing things. Their lives are enhanced by an increased frequency of contact with the outside world. Living in a harsh climate, Greenlanders have developed an effective form of communal organization to optimize survival.

> *There are three major stages in human values, which are linked to foraging, farming, and fossil-fuel societies…. [I]n each case, modes of energy capture determined population size and density, which in turn largely determined which forms of social organization worked best, which went on to make certain sets of values more successful and attractive than others.*
> *(Morris 2015, 139-140)*

As Greenlanders travel, their culture is modified. Young minds are influenced by life ways that are other than traditional. Locally, there are increasing levels of adaptation to western-style consumption. With more visitors within their own communities, local culture is modified.

**Face with Hood Ruff**
*Sheldon Richards (Innu).*
*Moose antler.*
*St. Carols, Newfoundland.*
*4" high x 3" wide.*

# Celebrations

We fear weather, hunger, cold, sickness. We fear the
souls of dead human beings and of the animals we have
killed….Therefore it is that our fathers have inherited
from their fathers all the old rules of life which are based on
the experience and wisdom of generations (Rasmussen
1930, 56). When at the end of life we draw our last breath,
that is not the end. We awake to consciousness again,
we come to life again, and all of this is effected through the
medium of the soul. Therefore it is that we regard the soul
as the greatest and most incomprehensible of all.

*Shaman Aua speaking to Knud Rasmussen near Melville Peninsula; Rasmussen 1930, 60.*

I n the multi-volume *Report of the Fifth Thule Expedition 1921–1924*,
Knud Rasmussen, a folklorist-ethnologist fluent in Inuktitut, who
was driven by unbounded curiosity and an insatiable curiosity about
the Inuit world and the intellectual culture of the Iglulik Eskimo,
was impelled to produce his 308 page ethnography from which the
above comments are quoted. It is now 16 years since 2002 when I first visited
Uummannaq. Until that time, my Arctic travel had been limited to Canada's
Inuit Territory. I am by no means a 'Rasmussen' nor do I hold claim to be
an ethnographer. Times change. Culture changes. But, whether on land, ice,
or water, many of the old ways recorded by Rasmussen still prevail, including
respect for the world of the spirit.

**Streetlights**
*Though picturesque, the December night was cold and blustery. The wind was so strong that I could not use a tripod. Rather, I leaned hard—camera firmly griped— into the side of a utility structure.*

I record below a celebration of life and community that we/I have been very fortunate to experience with our Greenlandic friends. In the Ilulissat/ Uummannaq region of northwest Greenland, Lindsay and I continued to experience a blend of Greenlandic and Scandinavian cultures, where a community holds a bright light to the Arctic night. Greenlanders love to socialize—especially during the "Dark Time", that is, the Arctic winter. High summer will do, too. The life ways of Greenlanders and Scandinavians are pleasurably, socially, and colorfully blended. As Rasmussen experienced throughout much of the north, celebrations and visits to members of a community are prized as a means to see winter through. These enhanced seasonal gatherings of family and friends are conducted over food, story telling, and just catching up.

*from top:*
**Promising warmth from within**
*While the church, constructed of quarried granite, did not
move with the wind, the imported Christmas tree, even anchored
by its wooden stand, was much in motion.*
**Christmas Eve Service**
*Although the service and choral music were conducted in
Greenlandic and Danish, Christmas joy included everyone.*

## Polar Night and Christmas

For more than a decade I was a frequent visitor to the Arctic for the summer
solstice, on the ice of Nunavut and, with Lindsay, in Nuuk, Greenland's
capital. But the winter of 2009/2010 was the first time that either Lindsay or
I had been in the Arctic for a polar night or winter solstice. We found winter
in Greenland pleasantly filled with warmth, not the harsh cold that we
expected five degrees north of the Arctic Circle. Glittering artificial light
streamed out through the windows of homes in Uummannaq. Light
cut through the Arctic night from the violet rays of streetlights and the
red, blue, and green of Christmas lights decorating nearly every home.

*left to right:*
**The Møller's Christmas celebration**
**Christmas lights**
*No house is without colored lights shining outward to the pleasure of neighbors and visitors.*

In the town center an imported tall, solitary Christmas tree stood next to the Lutheran church, both resplendent in white lights and with the light of a full moon adding to the brilliance of the Arctic night. Inside the church the women's choir, in traditional embroidered dress, sang hymns in Greenlandic, some of which were composed by Ludwig Hammeken's great grandfather. Through the tall Gothic-style windows, one could see occasional flashes of the northern lights streaming and flexing in the sky. On December 30 and 31 in Uummannaq, those northern lights are more likely to be fireworks exploding in the black river of the Arctic sky! For star watchers, the sparkling Milky Way can also be seen. From home to home, good cheer is celebrated through New Year's Day and beyond.

Even above 70° north latitude, the sky still plays its light on everything in the landscape. From beneath the horizon, sunlight reflects and refracts upward through atmospheric ice crystals to create layered bands of light, ranging from lilac to crimson. In the east, light travels laterally over the sea and out between the mountains whose mass defines the entrance to Uummannaq harbor. This wash of light illuminates the town from about 11:00 AM to 2:00 PM. For several hours on Christmas Day, this light—with only a little exaggeration—was so bright that it could have been a spring morning, though the temperature and ice on the harbor reminds us otherwise.

The sky was overcast for the next few days, reducing much of the visual
detail of the village and land. Strong winds knocked out both television and
internet transmissions. Oil lamps and candles were lit. At the end of
December, the temperature, amazingly, was 1° Celsius (34° Fahrenheit) in
Uummannaq, warmer than in much of Europe or North America. Local
sources told me that these higher temperatures started in the late 1990s. On
the last day of the year when the temperature might once have been minus
20° or 30° Celsius (-4 to -22° Fahrenheit), a strong, warm wind flowed from
the south. In Uummannaq's harbor, newly formed fast ice transformed into
expanding pools of water. The fjord became a giant ruddy liquid mirror.
On the last day of 2009, while it merely rained in Uummannaq, there was a
torrential downpour to the south in Nuuk, while not far to the north a
massive storm was forecast for the town of Upernavik. The Arctic's crazy
weather darkens.

In Uummannaq, Ann Andreasen and her staff always keep guests socially
engaged, with dinner invitations to her home or the to the homes of friends,
with adventures on land and sea, and with visits to the Children's Home.
What they call 'country food' across Baffin Bay in Nunavut is much the same
as it is in Greenland. At home in Maine, we very much enjoy the camaraderie
of small-town life. Even though we speak neither Greenlandic nor Danish,
we still experience much the same ease in Uummannaq. Here, these
bountiful meals from both sea and land include narwhal (*Monodon monoceros*)
which is served quite salty, halibut (*Reinhardtius hippoglossoides*), ringed seal

(*Pusa hispida*) which is served numerous ways, polar bear (*Ursus maritimus*) which is served as soup, Arctic char (*Salvelinus alpinus*), reindeer (*Rangifer tarandus*), muskox (*Ovibos moschatus*), Arctic hare (*Lepus arcticus*), ptarmigan (*Lagopus muta*), even caviar and scallops, both perhaps imported. Then there is a good complement of 'store food': Danish food and drink, fruit and nut pastries, sweet butter, tapioca-based whipped cream, Carlsberg beer, and Gammel Dansk bitters as well as a good selection of Cabernet from Pilersuisoq.

## Greenland National Day

Greenland National Day on June 21st has more than one purpose: it is also the first day of summer and Flag Day (with the flag displayed sun side up—be careful to do this). The Summer Solstice also commemorates Greenlanders lost at sea. They are remembered in Greenlandic churches by a model of a fishing boat suspended high over the main aisle of the church. The 2013 ceremony commenced near municipal offices in Uummannaq, then with a kaffemik inside its offices, then to church to give thanks and to remember the departed.

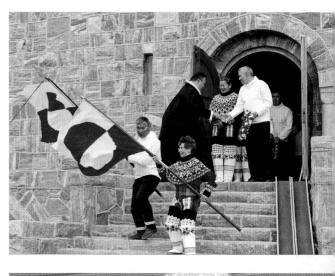

*clockwise from right:*
**Daughter of Uummannaq leads celebration**
*In June 2013, Greenland's Prime Minister Aleqa Hammond, at top of stairs, visiting Uummannaq where she was raised, leaves church after services in remembrance of Greenlanders lost at sea.*
**Greenland National Day**
*Greenland Day remembers those lost at sea through war as well as economic endeavors. In 2013, an American news team prepares to film a celebration at the local level in Uummannaq.*
**Commemorative Services**
*Remembrance of lives lost is attended by the community in the town's Lutheran Church.*

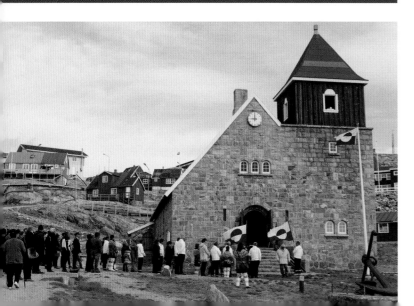

## 250th Anniversary

In July of 2013, Greenland's Prime Minister Aleqa Hammond cruised to Uummannaq on the Danish Naval vessel Tulugaq, an 'inspection ship' whose usual mission is to check that fishing boats are operating in compliance with Danish fishing regulations. The town was arrayed with indigenous crafts, musical concerts, dancing, clowns, bursting balloons, commemorative speakers, a display of Greenlandic skin boats and tools, and the municipal offices decorated with sealskins. Like a myriad of colorful fall leaves or an alpine field flowing with fresh, spring blossoms, the women of Uummannaq stand in vivid traditional dress. Comparison of this image with a black-and-white image taken about seven decades ago shows that traditional women's dress in Greenland remains unchanged. Ellen Christof-fersen, who had returned to Greenland after serving as a Parliamentarian in the Government of Denmark, demonstrated that she is not only an excellent speaker but also an energetic organizer. At the time of writing, Ellen had returned to Denmark. Later that day, a multi-course commemorative banquet of Greenlandic seafood and wines, specially labeled as 'Uummannaq 250 Vintage', was held with many other notables in attendance, including the officers from the Tulugaq.

*from top:*
**The Tulugaq**
*In July 2013, Prime Minister Hammond returned to Uummannaq in the Danish naval vessel, Tulugaq, to celebrate Uummannaq's 250th anniversary. Uummannaq is older than the United States.*
**Women of Uummannaq**
*Lined along the front of Uummannaq's municipal building, the town's women commemorate, in speech as well as in music and their national dress, the founding of Uummannaq.*

*from top:*

**Traditional West Greenland Women's Costume**
*This black and white image of women's traditional dress shows that little has changed in eight or nine decades. The west Greenland dress became the national dress, although east and north Greenland each has its own style. Image from Knudsen-Holm family archives used with permission.*

**Celebratory Dinner of Uummannaq's 250th Anniversary**
*At right head of table, Greenland PM Aleqa Hammond (seated far right) enjoys the evening at head table.*

**Fellow UPI Research Fellow Erik Torm and Ann's stepson Ludwig Hammeken**
*After dinner, we reconvened outside the auditorium for an extensive fireworks display.*

**Ann and Lindsay stand with officers of the Danish Naval ship, Tulugaq**
*Having served overseas on U.S. military ships, I was eager to see this Danish ship and talk with its officers and crew.*

*left to right:*
**Markussen kaffemik in the Hammeken residence in Nuuk**
*Up a flight of stairs to the apartment of Ole Jørgen Hammeken's mother, a well-attended kaffemik for a member of the Markussen family was underway. On the left, Mrs. Hammeken is featured in one of the most heart-warming images I have ever been privileged to share—smiles of guests are dazzling, babe in arms to complement Biblical lithograph on wall, all in perfect harmony.*
**Ole Jørgen Hammeken's nephew, sister, and mother**
*Greenlanders as they are!*
**The Markussen Family**
*Being accepted as more than a tourist is warmly communicated in these smiles, a wonderful gift.*

## Kaffemik—Tradition and Celebration

Kaffemik is like an open house. A classic event adopted from colonial times, it has become the most popular way in Greenland to celebrate life events. Literally translated, kaffemik means 'coffee and milk', but the fare is more like a banquet, a feast from cake to quiche to chewy narwhal and imported wine from the cellars of Pilersuisoq. Alas, grapes still are not grown in Greenland.

Kaffemik is an event held to celebrate a birth, birthday, death, graduation, confirmation, or any other occasion. All who wish to attend are welcome. On the first trip in which Lindsay accompanied me to Greenland, in 2004, we were invited to a kaffemik with Naja Rosing, her husband Kunuunnguaq Fleischer, and educator Erik Torm, to celebrate Naja's birthday. Fourteen years later Erik and I are now colleagues as UPI Research Fellows, while Kunuunnguaq and Naja have retired to Denmark. Over the succeeding years, as cradle-to-grave events have continued, so have the kaffemik to celebrate them. We retain the many friendships made at a succession of kaffemiks, on both a professional and personal basis. These are chance events happening at the right time and in the right place. Friendships begun at the kaffemik continue to expand.

*from top:*
**U.S. Fourth of July**
*What is more emblematic of the occasion, and resourcefulness of a friend, than finding hot dog rolls and baked beans in a land above the Arctic Circle to celebrate an American holiday?*
**Jonna, Ann, and Heidi with US signature "red, white, and blue" souvenir mementos**
*Greenland is a place where foreign guests are made to feel at home.*

## Fourth of July

René asked us how we celebrated the Fourth of July or Independence Day, in the United States. He added that we should celebrate it in Uummannaq with a feast of traditional American food that René particularly associates with the Fourth: barbecue, corn bread, and Boston baked beans. At the Children's Home, René, Lindsay, and others were busy over the stoves. Lindsay used canned beans to make Boston baked beans, which were savored as our own 'country food'. The baked beans quickly disappeared. Flags were made from images downloaded from the Internet and printed by laser, then assembled as red, white, and blue napkins. René fired up a huge, freestanding, metal-encased barbeque pit on which he barbecued spare ribs, hot dogs from the Pilersuisoq, American hamburgers, chicken wings, and pork and beans. Other food included cabbage and carrot salad, macaroni and cheese, homemade pastries and cookies, and ice cream. Finally, there was corn-on-the-cob—but canned—presented by our host Ann and her visiting Faeroe Island relatives in the best spirit of the 4th of July. The celebration was accompanied by popular music—European, Greenlandic, and American.

## Greenlanders in Maine and Washington, D.C.

From 2005 forward, visitors from Greenland and Denmark have frequently visited Maine, often in conjunction with visits to Washington, D.C. and New York. In conjunction with the Smithsonian Festival of Greenland, in May of 2005, an Arctic climate change symposium was held at the Royal Embassy of Denmark in Washington, DC. At both the festival and the symposium, I was delighted that I could present my images of Greenland. Other speakers at the symposium included Anders Fogh Rasmussen, later Prime Minister of Denmark and then NATO Secretary, and Robert Peary IV, who later traveled to the Eagle Island (Maine) home of his great grandfather Robert E. Peary. A group photo was taken at the Royal Embassy of

clockwise from left:

**Smithsonian Festival of Greenland 2005**

*The image on the banner that became the festival's logo, is a vertical slice of my photograph of the island community of Kangaamiut.*

**Anders Fogh Rasmussen at the Smithsonian's podium**

*His Excellency was then Prime Minister of Denmark, later to become Secretary General of NATO.*

**Robert Peary IV, Greenlandic descendant of Arctic explorer Robert E. Peary**

*After the Arctic Festival in Washington, Robert Peary came to Maine to visit the home of his namesake on Eagle Island, located south of Brunswick in Casco Bay.*

**Arctic Climate Change Symposium at Royal Embassy of Denmark**

*In photo, from left are: Will Richard; Bill Fitzhugh; His Excellency Friis Arne Petersen, the Ambassador of Denmark; and Aqqaluk Lynge, poet and former President of the Inuit Circumpolar Conference.*

**Peary-MacMillan Arctic Museum, Bowdoin College Campus, Brunswick, Maine**

*From left are Genevieve LeMoine, Arctic Museum Curator; René Kristensen; Ann Andreasen; Susan Kaplan, Museum Director and Archeologist; and, Ole Jørgen Hammeken.*

**Greenlanders come in numbers**

*While in Greenland in 2009, René mentioned to me that some Greenlanders would visit New York City in the fall and that they might visit Maine too. Of those who visited New York, fourteen visited us in Maine. Greenlanders love to travel in groups.*

*clockwise from top left:*

**A repeat visit by Greenlanders in 2010**
*We welcomed into our home a delightful blend of Green-landers and Mainers: Included were René Kristensen and Hans Gunnar, one of the young men from the Children's Home; Brent Perow, a friend and lobsterman in George-town; staff from the Chewonki Foundation who were co-hosts on the first trip of Greenlanders to Maine; and Inger Knudsen Holm Morse, husband Dr. Ed Morse; and, Inger's son Bill Holm.*

**Inger and Maine lobsterman Brent Perow**
*Both are storytellers and both had many stories to share.*

**Council of International Appalachian Trails in Halifax, Nova Scotia**
*During a visit to Nova Scotia by Greenlanders in 2010, council members studied maps of Greenland to determine where the proposed IAT trail would be located. A unani-mous vote welcomed Greenland as an IAT chapter.*

**René and Richard Anderson, IAT founder and President, look out on Mt. Katahdin**
*René would soon climb Mt. Katahdin, starting point for the IAT that would lead to Arctic lands of the North Atlantic.*

*top, left to right:*
**Greenland IAT chapter climbs Mt. Katahdin in 2010**
*After being outfitted at L.L. Bean store in Freeport, Maine,*
*the party set out to hike over Katahdin and beyond, to*
*the Canadian border where the IAT crosses into New*
*Brunswick. Hikers and packs are lined up at the Blue*
*Moose Restaurant in the trail town of Monticello, Maine,*
*to experience some Aroostook County food.*
*left:*
**Exploring the Eastern Inuit World**
*On her 2012 visit to Washington, DC, Ann Andreasen posed*
*with Abi Kristiansen, and my son Judd and his wife Clare.*

Denmark. Starting in the fall of 2009, Ann Andreasen, René Kristensen, and other Greenlanders from the Children's Home began regular visits to Maine. They were eager to view the Peary Arctic Centennial Exhibit at the Peary-MacMillan Arctic Museum at Bowdoin College in Brunswick. We were pleased to introduce our Greenlandic and Maine friends to each other at our home in Georgetown, Maine. The worlds of Greenland and Maine really came together on the occasion of a follow-up visit of Greenlanders in 2010: Inger from Jakobshavn (Ilulissat), Dr. Ed Morse, husband of Inger, René and Hans from Uummannaq, Inger's son Bill, Maine lobsterman Brent Perow, and Chewonki Foundation staff—a gathering of friends from the North Atlantic region, friendships without borders!

On their first visit to our home in 2009, Ann and René learned about the International Appalachian Trail (IAT) and made a commitment to establish an IAT chapter in Greenland. At a subsequent meeting of the Council of International Appalachian Trails in Halifax, Nova Scotia, in 2010, chapter representatives unanimously voted to approve establishment of a Greenland chapter. Upon seeing Maine's Mt. Katahdin for the first time, René (shown here with IAT founder Richard Anderson), determined to climb Katahdin,

which he accomplished in 2012 with a crew from the Uummannaq Children's Home. In turn, the following year, 2013, I joined René and a hiking party from Uummannaq across the Nuussuaq Peninsula on the Greenland portion of the IAT. (Also see Chapter 5-Current Economy).

Ann Andreasen, Abi Kristiansen, my son Judd, and his wife Clare posed with my work Exploring the Eastern Inuit World in the Smithsonian's Ripley Gallery at the 18th Biennial Conference of the Inuit Studies Association, October 2012. In May of 2015, at the Smithsonian's Arctic Spring Festival, hosted to recognize the US accession as Chair of the Arctic Council, Uummannaq sent the largest contingent from the Arctic. While there, Greenlanders presented an impromptu concert on the grounds of the Embassy of Denmark. Musician and composer Jean Michael LaVallee, a member of Ann's delegation, enjoyed the music along with one of the charges of the Uummannaq Children's Home. Among events at the Spring Festival was Jody Sperling's *Time Lapse Dance*, which was performed to music that emulates the sound of the sea and of ice in the Arctic. By coincidence, the day included a flyover of the Mall by a number of World War II military aircraft in celebration of the 70th anniversary of VE Day. Most recently, in July of 2015 in Brunswick, Maine, the Maine North Atlantic Development Office welcomed Inuuteq Holm Olsen, Greenland's first diplomatic representative to the United States. Inuuteq has since become a familiar presence in Washington and Reykjavik, Iceland.

Greenland, with its tradition of life-supporting community interdependency, and of people and place, embodies a cooperative culture. Even the dogs learn to cooperate. We of the West, with our craving for "I must have 'this' or 'that' thing, would do well to move in the opposite direction, from a competitive to a cooperative model. At a global level, we need to develop a similar interdependency if we are to successfully address the environmental degradation of our home, planet Earth. Indeed, thinking and acting 'beyond borders' is immensely gratifying.

from left:

**Greenland's Representative to the United States**

*Inuuteq Holm Olsen seated beneath an oak tree in Freeport, Maine.*

**Arctic Spring Festival**

*In 2015, Ann attended the Arctic Spring Festival with several residents of the Children's Home. At the festival, the United States accepted for the next two years the rotating Chair of the Arctic Council. Ann and her party presented a folk concert at the Danish Embassy.*

**Arctic Ice dancers**

*Electronic and acoustical music mimics the sounds of glacial movement and gushing of ice melt as the Jody Sperling dancers in diaphanous flowing veils transform into aquatic creatures of dark, ominous Arctic waters.*

**Inuit Looking Skywards**
*by Jimmy Uniukshayuk.*
*Caribou antler.*
*Pangnirtung, Baffin,*
*Nunavut. 4" high.*

# 10

# Looking Forward

[Like the bushmen hunter-gatherers of the Kalahari, the Inuit of the Arctic face] "...a rapidly changing polyglot modern state....But with thousands of years of living off the land, they possess a special, if ephemeral, double perspective on the modern world, one that comes from being in the world but of another; from being part of a modern nation-state yet simultaneously excluded from full participation in it; and from having to engage with modernity with the hands and hearts of hunter-gatherers.

*James Suzman. Affluence without Abundance: The Disappearing World of the Bushmen. (2017, 17).*

Climate change is uniquely long-term. The past decade was the warmest in human history. The one before was the second warmest. The one before that was the third-warmest...Changes are nowhere as evident as above the Arctic Circle: Arctic sea ice has lost half of its area and three-quarters of its volume in only the past thirty years.

*Gernot Wagner and Martin L. Weitzman. Climate Shock: The Economic Consequences of a Hotter Planet. (2015, 9).*

**Lichen – Uummannatsiaq**
*Life flourishes throughout Uummannaq Fjord,
as seen, for example, in the diverse forms of
rust-colored lichen found in Uummannatsiaq.*

The act of 'maintenance' does not mean holding on to a static condition. Rather, it means continuing the struggle to repair, to support, to safeguard, to nurture, and to advance. Warmer climate results in less seasonal and more erratic formation of sea ice. With less reliable ice conditions, seal, the primary source of protein and fat in the diet, is no longer so easily caught, as discussed earlier, and the human diet is compromised. Greenland is undergoing noteworthy change in its traditional food supply, from traditional foods to store bought items that may spawn western-type medical problems. To paraphrase Wagner and Weitzman, we cannot undue what had been climatically undone. Once glaciers and ice caps are gone, they cannot be reestablished by human action. "The severity of the problems will have been locked in by past actions, or lack thereof. Future generations will be largely powerless against their own fate" (Wagner and Weitzman 2015, 5).

With its images and narrative, this book characterizes the interdependency of the relationship between climate and culture. The advantage of using visual imagery to bridge a cross-cultural context is not unlike a NASA 'rover' sending back images of an extraterrestrial landscape, a goodly portion of which remains unknown. American writer and former Uummannaq resident, Gretel Ehrlich writes that '…we are pushing against the temple walls of sila'—a Greenlandic word, which simultaneously means climate, nature and consciousness (2004, 122, 179). Greenland is a huge place, stretching from the same latitude as northern Labrador to just seven degrees south of the North Pole, roughly a distance of 1,450km (900mi). Greenland is one-third larger than Alaska and fifty-one times the size of its mother country Denmark. Implicit in these quantifications is that there is more than one shared earth ecology or one cultural model for Greenland. For example, 'agriculture' as practiced by the Norse for 500 years eventually disappeared because of a decline in temperature brought about by climate change, and through degradation of the land by early settlers who stripped the land of its limited fecundity. In the south of Greenland, agriculture is once again being practiced with hay, sheep, and potatoes. Cucumbers are now being harvested at an experimental farm in southern Greenland for sale in Qaqortoq. To the north, through climate change and warming, an ice-based hunting culture is now at risk, perhaps to be supported in future by the mining of iron, gold, rare earth, and ruby deposits that have been discovered.

With Arctic warming and the associated shrinkage in the thickness and extent of fast ice, sea mammals such as narwhal and the polar bear are experiencing environmental stress, if not population declines. When there is ice cover, hunting of the orca, with its four-foot high dorsal fin, is limited. Today, narwhal face increased predation from orca that can now take advantage of reduced ice cover. With little ice, polar bears hunting in the open, wind-swept waters are drowning.

Meanwhile, the number of travelers to northern venues of Alaska has increased. These visitors wish to witness the physical expression of 'climate change'—seeing is believing. Paradoxically, climate change is not only an attraction for visitors, but makes it easier to visit because passage by both air

**Lichen—Telerua**

*Nature carved this pattern on Telerua Island through the water-driven erosion of granite; a species of orange lichen proclaims its beauty.*

*from top:*
**Instant composition—Uummannaq Fjord**
*Perhaps I am the only human to see from a helicopter this drifting, momentary composition of ice shaped by shifting winds and water.*
**'Sleeping Woman'—Karrat Island**
*Carved from rock on Nuugaatsiaq's Karrat Island is 'Sleeping Woman,' her hair cascading into its reflection. With its grand sweep of mountains, American painter Rockwell Kent was greatly attracted to Karrat as a primary venue of his work in Greenland in the early 1930s.*

and water has become less daunting. Simultaneously, the technocratic culture of the west is impacting traditional Greenlandic culture in terms of consumer expectations influenced by television, social media, and the Internet. Figuratively, distance is diminished. Rather than perish from cold and storm, a hunter stranded on the ice with his dogs can use his cell phone to call a rescue station, and then wait for help.

Visitors from abroad also have an impact, and western culture is gradually being mainstreamed into Greenlandic culture. For instance, dancing to country and western music at local bars or listening to the *Grand Ole Opry* have become as ingrained as use of such expressions as 'OK'.

Traditional subsistence and hunting cultures survived by not over exploiting the land, and their populations needed to be mobile and live in small numbers. Colonial powers, followed by various adventurers, followed by business people, and then by modern tourists, challenged and displaced the millennia-long cultural ways of a seasonal movement that had been driven historically to seek food from the sea through skillfully developed hunting techniques. Over the last few generations, Inuit peoples have experienced their own Neolithic ('agricultural') Revolution, except in this case it is called 'store-bought' food. The trend is to increased population concentrations in settled places, which become fossil-fueled outposts of the western world.

Families and other small groups scattered around Uummannaq Fjord require social services (health care, education, housing) as well as petroleum products, replacement parts and other necessities, and food other than that acquired by hunting and gathering. In turn, infrastructure for transportation and communication with the outer world has been established and people have been trained to service them. These associated, and accelerating, costs of a market economy are passed on to those Greenlanders who obtain their livelihood largely outside the cash economy but who have become increasingly dependent on the market economy. This is a classic dilemma posed by the centrally planned development of traditional cultures.

One result of connections fostered with the outside world is migration from settlements to larger, central places with more of a market economy, places such as Qaqortoq, Narsaq, Nuuk, Maniitsoq, Sisimiut, Aasiaat, Ilulissat, and Uummannaq (Map 1) as well as beyond Greenland to Denmark and other countries. Simultaneously, there is at least *de facto* government encouragement to leave subsistence settlements and move to more central places. This regional loss of population, usually of the young, is an important migratory pattern that has occurred in other northern cultures—for example, Newfoundland, Labrador, Quebec, Maritime Canada, even my own home State of Maine—that were largely dependent on the land and/or sea for survival (Wenzel 1999, Brody 2000, Morrisey 2005, Kuhnlein and Receveur 2007). In many cases, costs to deliver goods and services to remote settlements are rising dramatically, particularly the cost of fossil fuels. These costs have become economically prohibitive to governments, sellers, distributors, and settlements.

Fortunately, there are thoughtful, enlightened leaders who, facing the changes wrought by the cash economy and changes to the environment, work to maintain community ways of life. There are entrepreneurs such as Jens and Bente Larsen, co-owners of *Airzafari*, and Erik Bjerregaard, Managing Director of the Arctic Hotel, who deliver world-class services. There is Pierre Auzias, who promotes the production and sale of Greenlandic art and who teaches at the Children's Home in Uummannaq. There are the traditional hunters like Unartoq, who continues to practice and teach the old ways. There are government-funded institutions such as Børnehjemmet—all of which ensure the continuation of indigenous culture while incorporating the best from Euro-American culture.

**Ice, sledges, dogs and drivers—
Uummannaq Fjord**
*There is pleasure in observing the
harmonization of human activity
with the art of nature.*

Cultural endeavors by the Children's Home include production of films; travel to places such as New York City and Washington, D.C.; hiking and summer camps in Maine and British Columbia (Canada); active participation in dog sledging, fishing, and hunting; environmental awareness; active instruction in Greenlandic as well as popular and classical music; and other art forms. The program of the Children's Home represents a deep pedagogic commitment by the Government of Greenland to that and other similar institutions, a promise that means a commitment of two decades or even more to each individual life. That commitment includes literacy and numeracy but also language training as well as an apprenticeship to one's own culture. It is an exposure to the arts and to foreign travel to Europe, the United States, Canada, Africa, and South America as well.

Four factors impelled me to write this book. First, I wanted to document with words and images the human-fueled climate disaster that awaits the planet. Second, I wanted to produce an integrated and coherent record of my Greenland travels. Third, this record or book is my way of saying 'thank-you' to all of my Greenlandic friends. Fourth, these thoughts and images are intended to introduce the reader, and the visitor to Uummannaq, to its

spectacular, pristine, Arctic complexion, and to its people who live, play, work and laugh here, who graciously and generously welcomed me into their world. With a special connection to Uummannaq, I have been fortunate to share in the culture and place of these northern people. With my wife Lindsay, with my friend René, and with many other gracefully accommodating Greenlanders, I have experienced travel by dog sledge and boat among the ice floes, hiked the mountains, bivouacked on the sea ice, visited islands, and dined on seal, narwhal, polar bear, and other foods, on the ice and in settlement homes.

In Chapter 1, I used a quote from Arctic anthropologist Frederica de Laguna. In closing, I again reference the words of Dr. de Laguna, in closing I again reference the words of Dr. de Laguna, and these are words that haunt my ability to do justice to the Uummannaq community. That extensive use of imagery closes the fissures between words:

> *How little can one keep of such an experience? One cannot express what was once real and living. That is incommunicable, and to try to force such an experience into words is to kill it (1977, 257).*

Still, in Arctic places such as Uummannaq that have experienced neither the Agricultural nor the Industrial Revolution, we can revive our ancient intimacy with nature—a close relationship that has been torn asunder by our self-imposed displacement from nature. Or, perhaps from this very nature, our subconscious gropes to reconnect with tens-of-thousands of years of practice in which humans remained as one with nature. I believe that our need to vacation (to 'vacate' one's daily life and economic identity) in mountain or seashore, forested or glaciated ecosystem—or our inclination to care for the garden or house plants; see the stars, sunrise, and sunset; keep pet animals; become birders; enjoy an open fire at night, and to be with unfettered nature – is an awakening to subconscious signals conveyed by our genetic code at least since the Paleolithic. As Knud Rasmussen summarized after the Fifth Thule Expedition: "It is good sometimes to feel the power of Nature over one. You bend in silence and accept the beauty without words (Cole 1999, xvi). And, more recently Hillary Rosner concludes that:

> *Research shows that interacting with nature affects us deeply—for the better. A connection to nature, even at an unconscious level, may be a fundamental quality of being human (2016, 74).*

*from left:*

**Moon prepares to set over Uummannaq**
*Awash in the subdued red of twilight, this full moon begins to seat itself at dusk on Uummannaq's skyline.*

**Dr. Edward Morse and Bill Holm – Owl's Head**
*For many years, my wife Lindsay and I would drive to Owl's Head in Maine each spring and fall for our semi-annual indoor picnic with Dr. Edward Morse and Inger Knudsen Holm. Inger passed away in 2013. Ed passed in 2016. This image is the last portrayal of Ed, here with his stepson Bill Holm in 2015.*

Knud Rasmussen became the iconic real-life image of man in harmony with the unforgiving nature of the north. As quoted by Bill Holm, son of Inger Knudsen Holm Morse—Rasmussen, the 'Father' of this northern land Greenland—choose to keep life simple:

> *"Give me dogs. Give me snow. And, you can have all the rest."*

Sadly, Ed, at age 98, passed on September 30, 2016 at his home in Owl's Head, Maine.

We of this developed, high-energy, material-choking, climate-threatening world miss the simplicity of nature with its rhythms from whence we came. We must deliberately find our place again within this earth if we as a species are to continue. As individuals, we must each consciously choose to live life more as an active, involved citizen of Planet Earth, rather than that of a passive, mindless consumer of the earth that sustains us. Humanity's hope requires a return to the 'drawing board' of wilderness as practiced by those cultures that continue to remain close to nature.

## Selected Sources

*Note: Entries in the Bibliography are intended to serve as an introduction to Greenland, and to the Arctic in general. Publications listed are in English. There are many other excellent works on Greenland in Danish.*

Abram, David
1997 *The Spell of the Sensuous.* NY: Vintage Books.

*Arctic.* University of Calgary Fellows.
1996 Count Eigil Greve Knuth 1903 – 1996, December. 401-403. 1997.

Bolster, W. Jeffrey
2012 *The Mortal Sea: Fishing the Atlantic in the Age of Sail.*
Cambridge, Massachusetts: The Belknap Press of Harvard University Press.

Box, Jason
2016 April 12 Another Greenlandic friend "Nuuk is close to drowning in water caused by rain and melted snow."
Jason Box @ climate_science.

Brown, Stephen R.
2015 *White Eskimo: Knud Rasmussen's Fearless Journey into the Heart of the Arctic.*
Boston: Da Capo Press.

Brody, Hugh
2000 *The Other Side of Eden: Hunters, Farmers, and the Shaping of the World.*
New York: North Point Press.

Canada. Fisheries and Oceans
June 4, 2015. Myth: There is no market for seal products. *Myths and Realities of the Seal Market.*
http://www.dfo-mpo.gc.ca/fm-gp/seal-phoque/myth-eng.htm

Cole, Terrence
1999 Introduction to *Knud Rasmussen Across Arctic America: Narrative of the Fifth Thule Expedition.* (1927). Classic Re-print Series No. 6. Fairbanks, Alaska: University of Alaska Press.

Collins, Jr., Henry B.
1946 *Anthropology During the War.* "American Anthropologist" 48 (1): 141–144.

Cornwallis, Grame, and Deanna Swaney
2001 *Iceland, Greenland & the Faroe Islands.* London: Lonely Planet Publications.

de Laguna, Frederica
1977 *Voyage to Greenland: A Personal Initiation into Anthropology.*
New York: W.W. Norton & Company, Inc.

Denmark National Space Institute. DTU Space. Technical University
      of Denmark
2015 *Ilulissat Climate Days*. Ilulissat, Greenland. June 2 – 5.

Diemberger, Kurt
2015 (1994) *Spirits of the Air*. Translated by Audrey Salkeld. First published in
Italy 1991. Great Britain and United States. Digital production Vertebrate
Digital, an imprint of Vertebrate, 2015. Sheffield, England © 1999 Kurt
Diemberger

Ehrlich, Gretel
2001 *This Cold Heaven: Seven Seasons in Greenland*. New York: Pantheon Books.

Ehrlich, Gretel
2004 *The Future of Ice: A Journey into Cold*. NY: Pantheon Books.

Eiseley, Loren
1957 (1946) *The Immense Journey*. New York: Vintage Books.

Encyclopedia Britannica
http://www.britannica.com/topic/Inugsuk-culture

Erwin, John C.
2004 *Arctic* 57 (2): 214–215.

European Commission
October 26, 2015 *Commission re-authorizes Greenland and Nunavut under the
Inuit Exception.*
http://ec.europa.eu/environment/biodiversity/animal_welfare/seals/seal_hunt-
ing.htm

Fagan, Brian
2000 *The Little Ice Age: How Climate Made History 1300 – 1850.*
NY: Basic Books.

Fitzhugh, William W.
1984 *Paleo-Eskimo Cultures of Greenland*. In "Handbook of North American
Indians", Vol. 5: 528 – 539. Smithsonian Institution: Washington, D.C. U.S.
Government Printing Office.

Fitzhugh, William W. and Wilfred E. Richard
2014 *Maine to Greenland: Exploring the Maritime Far Northeast*. Washington,
DC: Smithsonian Books.

Fitzhugh, William W. *Personal communication.*
2015 January 23.

Flannery, Tim
2005 *The Weather Makers*. New York: Atlantic Monthly Press.

Freuchen, Peter
1953 *Vagrant Viking: My Life and Adventures*. New York: Julian Messner, Inc.

Fritz, Hermann
2017 https://ce.gatech.edu/news/after-recon-trip-researchers-say-greenland-tsunami-june-reached-300-feet-high. September.

Gènsbøl, Benny
2004 *A Nature and Wildlife Guide to Greenland*. Copenhagen: Gyldendal Publishers.

Gotfredsen, Anne Birgitte and Tinna Møbjerg
2004 *Nipisat – a Saqqaq Culture Site in Sisimiut, Central West Greenland*. In Man and Society (Meddelelser om Grønland).

Government of Greenland
2007 *Founding Statement*. Uummannaq Polar Institute 2007.

Graham, Alastair G.C.
2011 *Ice Sheet*. In "Encyclopedia of Snow, Ice and Glaciers", edited by Vijay P. Singh, Pratap Singh and Umesh K. Haritashya, 592 – 607. The Netherlands: Springer Books.

Greene, Mott T.
2015 *Alfred Wegener: Science, Exploration, and the Theory of Continental Drift*. Baltimore, Maryland: Johns Hopkins University Press.

Greenland
2013 *Greenland in Figures*. Statistics, Greenland. Nuuk, Greenland.

Grønnow, Bjarne, Jens Fog Jensen; Christy Ann Darwent
2003. *The Northernmost Ruins of the Globe: Eigil Knuth's Archaeological Investigations in Peary Land and Adjacent Areas of High Arctic Greenland*. Copenhagen: Danish Polar Center.

Hallendy, Norman
2000 *Inuksuit: Silent Messengers of the Arctic*. Vancouver, BC: Douglas & McIntyre Ltd.

Hansen, Hart, Jens Peder, Jørgen Meldgaard, and Jørgen Nordqvist (eds.).
1991 (1985). *The Greenland Mummies*. London: British Museum Press.

Hansen, James
2015 *Ice Melt, Sea Level Rise, and Superstorms. Evidence from Paleoclimate Data, Climate Modeling, and Modern Observations that 2° C Global Warming is Highly Dangerous*. http://www.slate.com/blogs/the_slatest/2015/07/20/sea_level_study_james_hansen_issues_dire_climate_warning.html?wpsrc=fol_fb

Hansen, James
2015 *Atmospheric Chemistry and Physics*. July 23.www.atmos-chem-phys-discuss.net/15/20059/2015.

Hastrup, Kirsten
2016 *Knud Rasmussen: Explorer, Ethnographer, and Narrator*. In "Early Inuit Studies: Themes and Transitions, 1850s - 1980s", edited by Igor Krupnik, 111 – 135. Washington, DC: Smithsonian Institution Press.

Holtved, Erik
1944 *Archaeological Investigations in the Thule District, Vol I*. Descriptive part. Meddelelser om Grønland, vol. 141, no. 1. Copenhagen.

Holtved, Erik
1944 *Archaeological Investigations in the Thule District, Vol II*. Analytical part. Meddelelser om Grønland, vol. 141, no. 2. Copenhagen.

Huntford, Roland
2001 (1997) *The Explorer as Hero*. London: Abacus (Little, Brown and Company).

Huston, James
1995 *Confessions of an Igloo Dweller: Memories of the Old Arctic*. New York: Houghton Mifflin Company.

Jackson, Michael
1995 *At Home in the World*. Durham, North Carolina: Duke University Press.

Jamieson, Dale
2014 *Reason in a Dark Time: Why the Struggle Against Climate Change Failed – and What It Means for Our Future*. NY: Oxford University Press.

Jordan, Richard H.
1984 In *Handbook of North American Indians*, Vol. 540-548. "Neo-Eskimo Prehistory of Greenland".
Smithsonian Institution: Washington, D.C. U.S. Government Printing Office.

Kahn, Brian
2016, April 12 *Greenland's Melt Season Started Nearly Two Months Early* in "Climate Central." www.climatecentral.org/news/greenlands-melt-season.

Kankaanpää, Jarmo
1996 *Thule Subsistence*. Doctoral Thesis. Providence, Rhode Island: Brown University. Research Gate. www.researchgate.net/publication/268332700

Kavenna, Joanna
2005 *The Ice Museum: In Search of the Lost Land of Thule*. NY: Viking Penguin.

Kipling, Rudyard
1895 (circa) "Ghost Dog (Quiquern)" in *The Second Jungle Book*. The Macmillan Company of Canada and Doubleday and company, Inc. Reprinted by permission of Mrs. George Bambridge.

Kissinger, Henry
2014 *World Order*. NY: Penguin Press.

Klein, Naomi
2014 *This Changes Everything: Capitalism vs the Climate*. NY: Simon & Schuster.

Knudsen Holm Morse, Inger and Edward K. Morse
2012 *Growing Up in Greenland*. Self-published with Charles and Christine Chamberlain.

Kolbert, Elizabeth
2006 *Field Notes from a Catastrophe: Man, Nature and Climate Change*. New York: Bloomsbury Books.

Kolbert, Elizabeth (ed.)
2007 *Introduction* in "The Ends of the Earth: An Anthology of the Finest Writing on the Arctic". NY: Bloomsbury Books.

Kolbert, Elizabeth
2014 *The Sixth Extinction: An Unnatural History*. New York: Henry Holt and Company.

Krupnik, Igor et al
2010 *SIKU: Knowing Our Ice: Documenting Inuit Sea-Ice Knowledge and Use*. NY: Springer.

Krupnik, Igor (ed.)
2016 *Early Inuit Studies: Themes and Transitions, 1850s – 1980s*. Washington, DC: Smithsonian Institution Press.

Kuhnlein, Harriet V., and Olivier Receveur
2007 *Local Cultural Animal Food Contributes Huge Levels of Nutrients for Arctic Canadian Indigenous Adults and Children*. In "The Journal of Nutrition" 2(April) 137: 1110–1114.

Laursen, Dan
1996 *Eigil Greve Knuth 1903 – 1996.* "Arctic" 49 *(4): 401–403.*

Lopez, Barry
1987 (1986) *Arctic Dreams: Imagination and Desire in a Northern Landscape.*
NY: Bantam Books.

Lopez, Barry
1998 *About This Life: Journeys on the Threshold of Memory.* NY: Random House.

Lüdecke, Cornelia
2003 *Lifting the Veil: The Circumstances that Caused Alfred Wegner's Death on the
Greenland Icecap.* Cambridge.) University Press, Cambridge Journals (1930)
Online. Polar Record, Vol. 36 / Issue 197 (April):139-154.

Mastny, Lisa
2000 (Updated November 4, 2015) *Coming to Terms with the Arctic* in
"World Watch Magazine". 13(1).
http://www.worldwatch.org/node/482

Mathiassen, Therkel
1927 *Archaeology of the Central Eskimo.* 2 vols. "Report of the Fifth Thule
Expedition 1921 – 1924". Vol.4(1 -2). Copenhagen.

Mathiassen, Therkel
1930 *An Old Eskimo Culture in West Greenland: Report of an Archeological
Expedition to Upernavik.* Geographical Review 20 (4): 605–614.

Mathiassen, Therkel
1931 *Ancient Eskimo Settlements in the Kangâmiut Area.* Meddelelser om
Greenland 91(1). Copenhagen.

Mathiassen, Therkel
1931 *Inugsuk, a Mediaeval Eskimo Settlement in Upernavik District, West
Greenland.* Meddelelser om Greenland 77(4):147-340. Copenhagen.

McCoy, Roger M.
2006 *Ending on Ice: The Revolutionary Idea and Tragic Expedition of
Alfred Wegner.* Oxford: Oxford University Press.

Meldgaard, Jørgen
1977 *The Prehistoric Cultures in Greenland: Continuity and Discontinuity in the
Inuit Culture of Greenland.* Hans P. Kylstra, ed. Groningen, The Netherlands:
University of Groningen Arctic Center.

Morris, Ian
2015 *Foragers, Farmers and Fossil Fuels: How Human Values Evolve*. Princeton, New Jersey: Princeton University Press.

National Snow and Ice Data Center
2016, April 12 Early start to Greenland Ice Sheet melt season. nsidc.org/ Greenland-today/

Nordhaus, William D.
2015 *A New Solution: The Climate Club*. Review of "Climate Shock: The Economic Consequences of a Hotter Planet" in
The New York Review of Books (LXII:10. June 4).

Pelto, Mauri
2008 *What Links the retreat of Jakobshavn Isbrae, Wilkins Ice Shelf and the Petermann Glacier?* http://www.realclimate.org/index.php/archives/2008/10/ what-links-the-retreat-of-jakobshavn-isbrae-wilkins-ice-shelf-and-the-petermann-glacier/#sthash.ZFL4IOCO.dpuf

Rasmussen, Knud
1927 (1999) *Across Arctic America: Narrative of the Fifth Thule Expedition*. Classic Re-print Series No. 6. Fairbanks, Alaska: University of Alaska Press.

Rasmussen, Knud
1930 *Intellectual Culture of the Iglulik Eskimos (Report of the Fifth Thule Expedition 1921 – 1924)*. Vol 7, Number 1.
Copenhagen: Gyldendalske Boghandel.

Richard, Wilfred E. and Michael John Willis
October 10, 2015 *Ilulissat Climate Days, Ilulissat Greenland*. June 1 – 5, 2015. Unpublished manuscript.

Rosner, Hillary
2016 *All Too Human: Would we want to live forever (if we could)?* "Scientific American" 315:3. 70 – 75 September.

Ruddiman, William F.
2005 *Plows, Plague, and Petroleum*. Princeton: Princeton University Press.

Safina, Carl
2011 *The View from Lazy Point: A Natural Year in an Unnatural World*. NY: Henry Holt and Company.

Sanguya, Joelie and Gearheard, Shari
2010 *Preface* in "SIKU: Knowing Our Ice: Documenting Inuit Sea-Ice Knowledge and Use". NY: Springer.

Scherman, Katharine
1956 *Spring on an Arctic Island*. Boston, MA: Little, Brown and Company.
Pp. ix – x.

Schiermeir, Quirn
2017 Nature: International Weekly Journal of Science. September 2017.
https://www.nature.com/news/huge-landslide-triggered-rare-greenland-
mega-tsunami-1.22374

Schledermann, Peter
1996 *Voices in Stone: A Personal Journey into the Arctic Past*. Calgary: The Arctic
Institute of North America, Komatik Series, Number 5.

Scranton, Ray
2015 *Tourists at the End of the World*. In "The Nation". 301(19): 12 – 21.
Smithsonian National Museum of Natural History
No date. David Littschwager, https://ocean.si.edu/ocean-acidification

Serreze, Mark C.
2018 *Brave New Arctic: The Untold Story of the Melting North*. Princeton, NJ:
Princeton University Press.

Sørensen, Af Mikkel and Kristoffer Buck Pedersen
2005 *Killiaq kilden p Nuussuaq: på poret af Saqqaqkulturens redskabssetn*
in "Greenland" March. Number 2-3. Published by the Greenland Society.

Suzman, James
2017 *Affluence without Abundance: The Disappearing World of the Bushmen*.
NY: Bloomsbury Publishing PLC.

Taylor, Arnold H.
2011 *The Dance of Air & Sea: How Oceans, Weather, & Life Link Together*.
NY: Oxford University Press, Inc.

The Guardian
May 16, 2015 *Inuit hunters' plea to the EU: lift seal cull ban or our lifestyle will be
doomed*.
http://www.theguardian.com/world/2015/may/16/greenland-inuits-urge-eu-
reverse-seal-ban-save-way-of-life

*Thule Archives – Book of Days Tales*. http://www.bookofdaystales.com/tag/thule/

UNESCO
2009 *Climate Change and Arctic Sustainable Development: Scientific, Social, Cultural,
and Educational Challenges*. Paris, Editor Peter Bates. France: UNESCO.

Wagner, Gernot and Weitzman, Martin L.
2015 *Climate Shock: The Economic Consequences of a Hotter Planet*. Princeton, New Jersey: Princeton University Press.

Weaver, Ray
2013 *Environment groups OK Greenland seal hunt*. "Arctic Journal". November 11. http://arcticjournal.com/culture/241/environment-groups-ok-greenland-seal-hunt

Wegener, Alfred and John George Anthony Skerl
1924 *The Origin of Continents and Oceans*. London: Methuen & Co.

Wegener, Alfred
1912 *Die Herausbildung der Grossformen der Erdrinde (Kontinente und Ozeane), auf geophysikalischer Grundlage. Petermanns Geographische Mitteilungen (in German) 63: 185–195, 253–256, 305–309*. Presented at the annual meeting of the German Geological Society, Frankfurt am Main (January 6, 1912).

Wegener, Alfred
1915 *The Origin of Continents and Oceans*. Translation by John Biram of the 4th edition (1928) of *Die Entstehung der Kontinente und Ozeane*. New York: Dover Publications (Revised 1966).

Wegener, Else (ed.)
1939 *Greenland Journey: The Story of Wegener's German Expedition to Greenland in 1930 – 1931*. As Told by Members of the Expedition and the Leader's Diary. Winifred M. Deans (trans.) London: Blackie & Sons.

Wenzel, George
1991 *Animal Rights, Human Rights: Ecology, Economy and Ideology in the Canadian Arctic*. Toronto: University of Toronto Press.

Wilson, Edward O.
1999 *Consilience: The Unity of Knowledge*. NY: Vintage Books.

Wilson, Edward O.
2014 *The Meaning of Human Existence*. NY: Liveright Publishing Corporation.

# Acknowledgements

This publication was made possible through the efforts of Lindsay Dorney, my wife, and Ronald Levere, my friend. Lindsay proofread for logical flow, argument, syntax, and grammatical structure. Bill Gasperini, Russian Arctic journalist, kindly conducted an initial read. Long-time friend Chris Clarkson is a stickler for detail; together in 2016, we generated the first complete draft of the manuscript. Bill Duffy produced the cartography. Through Ann Andreasen, Director of the Uummannaq Polar Institute, frequent commercial travel to Greenland was provided. Through Renee Crain, US National Science Foundation Program Manager for Arctic Research Support and Logistics, flights were made available with the Air National Guard 109th between Stratton Air Force Base of Scotia, New York and International Science Support Services in Kangerlussuaq, Greenland. I particularly thank my colleague William Fitzhugh of the Smithsonian National Museum of Natural History who melded my worlds of artistry and northern travel into an Arctic-focused career, which now spans more than 20 years. He, Nancy Shorey and Chris Clarkson helped proofread.

Black and white images of the Uummannaq /Jakobshavn region over the second, third, and fourth decades of the Twentieth Century are from the family archives of Aage Knudsen, Kolonibestyrer (District Manager) of north Greenland for that period. His daughter Inger Knudsen Holm Morse maintained these archives and Inger's son William Morse, of Camden, Maine, graciously offered access to these family archives. Inger's brother Per Knudsen, of Copenhagen, Denmark, provided a narrative of some images used in this book.

*left to right:*
**Lindsay at home in Maine, Spring 2015. Our first kaffemik was in Uummannaq in 2004 for Naja Rosing with husband and very good friend Kunuunnguaq Fleischer (center), and future fellow UPI Research Fellow Erik Torm.**

Ulf Østerlund suffered a fatal fall while working on his home in Spain. We will miss him.

With the encouragement and generous assistance of Ann Andreasen, Kunuunnguaq Fleischer, and Inger Knudsen Holm Morse, this book as well as other related publications have been given birth. I wish to thank colleague René Kristensen for his generosity in the field in Greenland, for making travel arrangements, and for the enjoyment of his visits to our home in Maine. I thank those Greenlanders, Faroese, and Danes who generously shared their lives with me. This includes the following (Others who are not citizens of the Danish Realm are so noted.):

Enok Alatak, Rasmas Alatak, Ron Alvarez (Venezuela), Heidi Andreasen, Lis Arrevad, Pierre Auzias (France), Erik Bjerregaard, Marc Buriot (France), Ellen Christoffersen, Esben Christiansen, Jorgen Dahl, Jonna Faeroe, Karl Fleischer, Kunuunnguaq Fleischer, Hans and Sofie Grønvold, Hans Gundel, Ludwig Hammekin, Ole Jørgen Hammeken, Aleqa Hammond, Kristina Hammond, Lene Kielsen Holm, Jean-Michel Huctin (France), Alfred E. R. Jacobsen, Krister Jansson (Sweden), Frank Jensen, Lars Emil Johansen, Rebekka Jørgensen, Christian Keldsen, Annie Kerouedan (France), Jens Klemensen, Knudsen Kunuunnguaq, Joas Korneliussen, Helene "Abi"Kristiansen, Malik Kristensen, Jens Ploug Larsen and Bente Biilman Larsen, Jakob "Unartoq" Løvstrom, Lucia Ludvigsen, Albert and Else Lukassen, Jakob Markussen, Ole Møller, Svend and Katti Møller, Niels Mønsted, Hans Mørch, Jonas Nielsen, Paulus Nikolajsen, Jakob and Arnarlunguaq Nordstrøm, Ulf Østerlund, Birthe Pedersen, Lars Poort, Stefan Rahmberg, Naja Rosing, Jens Sigurdsen and family, Bolethe Skade, Barbara Strøem-Baris, Hans Thomassen, Erik Torm, Svend Zeeb.

# Contributions from the Field

# The Essence of Uummannaq

The Uummannaq Children's Home and
Uummannaq Polar Institute: It Takes a Village
to Raise a Child in Greenland Too

*Ann Andreasen and Jean-Michel Huctin*

Why many people around the world know of the small, northern remote island of
Uummannaq can be found in the activities of its Children's Home. Production of international films, concert tours in many countries and educational involvement of many foreign
friends are some of the activities designed to heal and raise children who come from
throughout Greenland with adverse childhood experiences. This residential center, which
operates under the auspices of Greenland's self-rule government, is located at the foot
of the island's signature mountain–Uummannaq.

How indeed to foster upbringing and education when a third of Greenlandic children admit
to facing school bullying, substance abuse, neglect and sexual abuse in unhealthy families?
How to raise and educate youth when some of them lack even the basic skills of forming
positive human relationships?

Working for decades with the most vulnerable children has given educators at Uummannaq
Children's Home concrete experience on how to succeed in these unbelievably bleak
circumstances and against all odds. Although success remains fragile, results are explained
in large part by the Home's educational philosophy that is inspired by Inuit traditional
knowledge as well as social work experience. The main ideas of this philosophy are to place
children always in the center to foster positive relationships between generations and in the
community. This structuring establishes an optimal nurturing environment through which to
become healthy adults.

A nurturing environment requires not only that children and teenagers with broken family
backgrounds live in a community providing them with formal opportunities to grow-up
but also that their community does not stigmatize this young cohort in any way. Therefore
the Uummannaq Children's Home has continued to practice for many years the ancient
African proverb popularized by the title and content of a book published in 1996 by Hillary
Clinton: it takes a village to raise a child.

## A Family-like home and the Uummannaq Polar Institute with culturally relevant and cross-cultural activities for children

Built in 1929 in Uummannaq, on the northwest coast of the island, the Children's Home—
in Greenlandic *Uummannami Meeqqat Angerlarsimaffiat*—is the oldest residential care center
for children in Greenland. With about 30 permanent residents under 23 years old (the

majority being teenagers), it has one of the largest contingents in the country of young people separated from their family because of neglect and abuse. While learning from professional caregivers the basics of a healthy and happy childhood that many were not fortunate to have before exposure at the Children's Home, each day offers life based on a family-like atmosphere where these residents feel secure and comfortable. Moreover, the Uummannaq Children's Home has developed original and exciting educational activities that are routed in the Greenlandic culture, both local and national, and open to our culturally globalized world of change and diversity. In 2007, the Uummannaq Polar Institute (UPI) was founded to stimulate these cross-cultural activities for youth, involving more foreign scientists, filmmakers and artists. More will be said later about the Home's sister institution, the Uummannaq Polar Institute.

## Fostering positive relationships between generations and within the community

The Home's educational environment is characterized by a regular presence of caring and competent, creative adults who boost cultural identity. Elderly people, who traditionally played an important educational role in the past Greenlandic society by raising children when parents could not do it, are included in the daily work with children at the Home. Who does not know the social worker Louise Zeeb, still around today after more than 50 years of dedication and excellent service? Who does not know the old hunter Jakob Løvstrøm, nicknamed Unartoq, still regularly employed as dogsled expert, boat pilot, and "informal educator"?

The Children's Home utilizes these human resources not only in its residences premises but also from the local community for daily activities or for special events in the school, sport hall, stores, streets and in private homes. For instance, successful youth graduating from school, winning sport games and giving away food to others when catching first seal or fish, (an old Inuit tradition), raise happiness and pride both in themselves and around them. Regular celebrations such as *kaffemik* (traditional open-house gathering where coffee/tea and cakes are served) for these kinds of events as for birthdays, first days in school, confirmation, weddings etc., present frequent opportunities to participate in community life, share respect, happiness and affection, and create positive relationships.

Importantly, to invite children and adults into the Children's Home encourages integration into the community, which avoids social marginalization and stigmatization while enhancing sense of place and identity. The so-called defects of a northern community 'to be small and remote' become an advantage: a nurturing educational environment for youth, easy access to nature, and offer the therapeutic affects of a peaceful people who know each other and who maintain solidarity of place. This is the kind of 'village' needed to raise children, especially those 'at risk'—as they are called in the US—separated from an abusive family context.

Local resources can be complimented by outside visitors who also 'make the village'. Greenlandic singer and songwriter Nivi Nielsen became a significant role model for Home residents. One of the girls followed in Ms Nielsen's tracks by writing her own songs, playing them live and recording a CD. Artists, filmmakers, sportsmen, scientists offer their time, their skills, their talents, and their equipment, to create specific educational activities available for the youth in Uummannaq. As Inuit culture attracts a lot of foreign people who wish to experience dog sledge rides and hunting trips. These guests are asked to share their talents and projects with young residents.

Integrated into the Children's Home daily life in Uummannaq or visiting one of the seven settlements in the bay, or even when together traveling abroad, these foreign friends contribute to creating a truly vibrant community. Examples include music teacher Jonna Færø from Faroe Islands, violinist and conductor Ron Davis Alvarez Lombano from Venezuela. Bluesman Guy Davis from the US helped Home residents feel good and proud by learning how to play musical instruments and to participate together in community concerts.

The reputation of the Children's Home outside Greenland is in large part due to these international guests and to the many films made in Uummannaq, inspired by emblematic educational activities with Greenlandic hunters in the Arctic wilderness. Filmmaking offers opportunities to promote personal positive perceptions among youth of their Greenlandic culture. The feature-length film *Inuk* (2012) was based on true stories of young residents from the Children's Home and professionally directed by screenwriters and young actors while shooting on scene locations. By re-enacting scenes inspired from their own lives in front of the camera, the film shooting was a special cathartic moment. Now, the film is out in theaters around the world.

Due to climate change worsening the thinning ice condition in Uummannaq that limits dog sled season and thanks to fortunate new opportunities, other educational activities have developed in the recent years. These include sports and adventures such as long-distance trekking in the mountains. Greenland is now part of the International Appalachian Trail, representing the only part of that trail which is located above the Arctic Circle. Social worker, educator, and hiker René Kristensen regularly guides teenagers during multi-day trips across high mountains and long valleys on the Appalachian Trail in Greenland's west Nuussuaq peninsula coast and in Maine USA. Hiking trips have even occurred through the Venezuelan jungle to reach the world's highest uninterrupted waterfall.

Through live music, Greenlandic artist Karina Møller is training a group of teenagers to perform traditional Inuit drum-dance and songs, accompanying them during beautiful shows in front of large audiences in many countries. This is another way of adapting to climate change while conceiving extremely exciting activities which interest young people and teach them skills and hope. These musical expressions are meant to be holistic because they bring together physical benefits as well as emotional, mental and spiritual ones to all the youth at the Uummannaq Children's Home and Polar Institute.

## Uummannaq Polar Institute

In 2007, the Uummannaq Polar Institute (UPI) was founded to support Arctic research by visiting scientists and to stimulate cross-cultural activities for youth, involving more foreign scientists, filmmakers and artists. Two years later, Prince Albert II of Monaco, together with French Arctic explorer and geo-anthropologist Jean Malaurie as well as Russian polar explorer and politician Artur Chilingarov visited Uummannaq to inaugurate the UPI.

One of the main 'lessons' of the educational experience at the Uummannaq Children's Home and at the Uummannaq Polar Institute is a simple truth that our most valuable resource is human, the positive relations that bond together young and old in the 'village' where we live, teaching us to respect and value each other, connecting us with the past, the present and the future, the closest and the furthest, the similar and the different. This is a simple truth that our busy individualistic life tends to forget today, although it could greatly improve the educational process and outcomes everywhere in the world.

We can summarize the action of Home and Institute in this way. Together, they bring together young residents with resourceful professional adults who share experiences through an exceptional diversity of socializing experiences. Together they make a contribution to each other's resilience and are beneficial to their integration into local and national communities.

Socializing experiences include culturally relevant activities such as dog sledding, hunting, fishing, and traditional outdoor life, which together foster personal and cultural well-being and pride. These experiences are markedly enhanced if they are mixed with other cross-cultural activities: travel to other countries, orchestral practice in concert, art therapy, filmmaking and sports. Together, they bring many different healthy benefits for the body and soul while learning non-formal skills that contribute to a meaningful life.

Therapy and education, combining traditional and western aspects, is essential for the individual to heal wounds, learn better and become comfortable with life in Uummannaq or anywhere in the world. Raising healthy and happy individuals is the fundamental prerequisite for development of a well-functioning, sustainable and self-ruled society in Greenland as well as participating in the mitigation efforts and adaptation to climate change. Here at the Children's Home and Polar Institute in North Greenland, we think globally when we act locally!

## REFERENCES

Andreasen, Ann and Huctin, Jean-Michell
2011. Children on Thin Ice, *Inter-Nord*, n°21, Jean Malaurie (ed.), CNRS, Paris.
Andreasen, Ann
2009. People on Thin Ice : The Need for Education and Research in Greenland, Climate
        Change and Arctic Sustainable Development: Scientific, Social, Cultural and
        Educational Challenges, UNESCO, Paris.
Christensen, Else; Kristensen, Lise G. and Baviskar, Siddhartha
2008. *Børn i Grønland, en kortlægning af 0-14-årige børns og familiers trivsel.*
        Copenhagen : SFI – Det National Forskningscenter for Velfærd.
Clinton, Hillary
1996. *It Takes a Village : And Other Lessons Children Teach Us.*
        NY, Simon & Schuster.
Gregersen, Conni
2010. *Livsmod : socialpædagogisk og psykoterapeutisk behandling af børn i Grønland,* Nuuk,
        Milik.
Huctin, Jean-Michel
2016. *Maltreatment and Well Treatment of Young People in Greenland from Traditional Inuit
        Education (17th-20th Centuries) to the Present Children's Home in Uummannaq,* PhD
        thesis in French (not published yet), University of Paris Diderot Paris 7.
Malaurie, Jean
1985. *The Last Kings of Thule,* University of Chicago Press.

# A Home at the Foot of the Heart-Shaped Mountain

*Esben Skytte Christiansen*

The Children's Home in the town of Uummannaq in the northwest of Greenland was originally built in 1929 as a sanatorium for sick children, children with sick parents or orphaned children. Since then the Children's Home has moved into newer and larger buildings. Here the children would be able to feel safe and at home. That is exactly why the Children's Home is furnished and equipped as a private home. And here things are done to create a good atmosphere to everybody's liking. This is the result of both the culture, expressed in the food, traditions, music and art, *the continuity*, creating the confidence that is so crucial, and the love the staff have for the children.

Child neglect and maltreatment have many faces. You encounter them all at the Children's Home in Uummannaq. The town population has during the last few decades been on decline, as it is the case in most places of the country. However, the children at the Children's Home come from all over the country, as the most difficult cases are well accepted here and because a special treatment method has been developed.

The children admitted here have not had even the most mediocre care, and the parents' and other family members' acts of abuse and violence are a recurring theme in each of these children's history. They have suffered serious losses, and other people having had the opportunity to intervene and help the children did not see them properly.

Many of the children have lost their hope when they arrive at the Children's Home in Uummannaq. The first period is a difficult time for most of them. The separation from the family is difficult, regardless of how neglected the children have been. However, joy and hope slowly win a place with every child at this exceptional residential home for children and young persons in the high north.

To provide the children with pride of their own culture and of the country's stunning scenery is essential to the work with these children. Therefore the Children's Home cooperates with local hunters who together with the staff teach the children how to be out in nature, teach them how to build sledges and how to look after the sledge dogs. It is necessary to master such skills on the long journeys with dog sledges, which are taking place every year. It is a part of the education all the children are receiving in order to get better independently in the harsh Greenlandic life.

A part of this education is also to know what is happening in other countries and cultures and how to get on there properly. Go out into the world you must, it gives your life a solid perspective. That is why travelling to other countries is an essential part of the Children's Home's educational method. Here the children often bring along their musical instruments, because all children at the Home learn how to play at least one instrument. On a daily basis the children are instructed by talented musicians and music teachers in order to be good enough to play for other people on their travels. In this way each child acquires a better self-confidence and gets experiences of how to enjoy other people by displaying his or her abilities. The experience of self-esteem, pride and joy is the goal; sledge rides, music and travel form a substantial part of the resources.

Many children first leave the Children's Home as adults and some never leave it entirely. When you have been failed and neglected in the very core of your personality and the network you have is mainly the one you have got at the Children's Home, there is a need to cling to the confident anchor, when life with its many challenges is a burden to the individual. It is called after-care and is of high priority for the Children's Home.

From the famous Danish fairy tale poet, Hans Christian Andersen's fairy tale "The Ugly Duckling," we know that the duckling suffered hardships, pain and failure. It was bullied, violated and abandoned. The story ends well, as the Ugly Duckling develops and gets a good life, but it will never forget the humiliation it experienced early in life.

The problem with child neglect and maltreatment is not solved just because 'the maltreatment' ceases. To get care at a children's home when you have lost your own family is only the beginning of the question: What do I do with my life?

It is not enough for the Ugly Duckling to find a swan family to get everything settled. It has been hurt in its history, which is imprinted in its memory. The duckling got a double trauma, as it has felt down and out no less than two times. The first battle happens in reality when the duckling is being pummelled in the duck yard. The second stroke hits when the imagination and the thoughts are being brought back to the first battle and gives it a sense of being humiliated and abandoned.

In order to cure the effects from the first stroke, a long-term healing process has to take place. In order to alleviate the pain of the second stroke it is necessary to change the image of what happened in reality at the first stroke; to change the picture of what was then done. The individual has to be able to imagine his or her misfortune and their course in a different way. Therefore the offer of caring for the individual is aimed for life. The children of the Children's Home should feel that they, in their pain, have been seen and been met with. And this gives them hope. It is precisely what the Children's Home in Uummannaq offers to the children who are so lucky to get there. "It doesn't matter about being born in a duck yard, as long as you are hatched from a swan's egg."—Or, you may add, if you are born in a battered family.

# Roots and Wings— Nationalization and Internationalization— Two Sides of the Same Coin

*Erik Torm*

It is wise to step carefully when cultural boundaries are exceeded. Although Greenland has a long history together with Denmark, and is heavily influenced by Danish culture through the centuries, there are basic cultural differences that cannot just be ignored, and which fundamentally characterizes our different ways of thinking and living. The Greenlandic schools have as a starting point in many respects been a copy of the Danish and it has meant that despite many both Greenlandic and Danish teacher's tenacious and often selfless work that the Greenlandic children often got a poor yield of teaching in the schools. With the 2002 reform (Landsting Regulation no. 8 of 21 May 2002) Greenland got a basic school education, which sought to build an education on the Greenlandic realities and expressed a vision of a school on a high professional level aiming to match the requirements of an ever more globalized world.

The elementary school reform had the intention to develop a school with roots in Greenlandic assumptions, but it was in reality more faithful to the Danish roots. The new professionalism in the curricula was based on theory of science and 'rationalistic' in its design. Spirituality and science were separated using the European style. And the school's everyday life was not organized in collaboration with culture and nature, in which it should unfold. Instead of getting a flexible school based on the Arctic culture and nature as the intention was, the school still remained an 'escape from reality'—a 'foreign body' with a school day split into classes, hours, subjects and lonely teachers and with a teaching practice that was an imitation of Danish school more than a locally based school.

The school's most important resource in this context is the teachers. It is the teachers who must provide all students with the challenges that make them knowledgeable and self-reliant, and that gives them self-esteem and belief in their own abilities.

Therefore the focus should be on teachers' continuous and lifelong learning. The fact that 25% of the teachers are uneducated (temporary teachers) can seem daunting, but it is also a fact that for many years to come it will not be possible to change. And the solution is not that teaching again should be dominated by summoned Danish or other foreign teachers. In a smaller scale teachers coming from abroad obviously are a good source of inspiration, but it should never become a pretext or a guiding factor in the teaching staff. The fact is that the school at the moment has to be developed using a large percentage of uneducated players on the field. Many of these temporary teachers show a lot of pride in their work with children. What they are missing is pedagogical and didactic knowledge and experience. Innovation projects show that it can easily be addressed if it is done on the spot and in close interaction between teachers and temporary teachers and with empathy in local conditions by the advisors/instructors. It is about being present in the local community and the school in periods of at least one week, preferably more.

There is obviously a difference whether we are talking about settlements or cities. In the big city schools, for example in Uummannaq, the teacher group is professionally broader and the foundation for professional sparring and development with colleagues is present. They just need to learn to take advantage of this, if they are not doing so, which in fact is already the case in several schools. For settlement schools with few teachers, of which some are uneducated, the situation is completely different. Often there is a lack of professional skills, because 2-6 teachers rarely will be able to cover all professional requirements as the curriculum prescribes. There is a need to develop other teaching methods such as exchange teachers and guest teachers in some periods and distance learning over the internet in other periods. We know that it is possible to implement both pedagogical and technological concepts, and we have experienced that settlement students are knowledge-eager and ready to learn when the challenges are exciting enough and the relationship with their environment exists.

To implement both pedagogical and instructional technology reforms takes time. This fact can unfortunately lead to a situation that the concerns themselves cause a delay in the development process so that reforms will take longer to implement than desirable because of uncertainty and fear of the new opportunities paralyzing organizations and decision makers. However it is obvious, when you look at the Greenlandic school history over the last 30 years, that the Greenlandic education system has undergone a change that differs substantially from developments in the former colonized areas or among other indigenous groups in the United States, Canada, Australia, New Zealand, etc.

Looking at higher education after primary school, it can be concluded that where Denmark did not succeed, in either as colonial power or as administrator of the Greenlandic education system, the Greenland Home Rule managed to change. Thus, over the last 30 years in which Home Rule has existed, we have created high schools, vocational high schools and a lot of other vocational and technical schools around the country created. Furthermore, we have created a University of Greenland where higher education gradually is being developed—just to mention some more tangible examples.

It is said that school and education must develop integrated human beings. If this shall have any meaning it has to be based in the diversity of the Arctic culture and nature. Therefore, school and education has to be linked to the culture and nature in the surrounding society. The flexible school and education can and must ensure that there is both a 'summer camp' and a 'winter camp' for the rising generation.—The diversity of life based on the Arctic realities becomes that way a forming force for a national Greenlandic education. These are the *roots*. The curricula and training content must then be the wings, carrying children and young people—and society—to be equal partners in the globalized world. But the curriculum must also be rooted in the cultural and historical reality. An integrated person in a globalized world needs to have both *'Roots and Wings'*.

# Jakob Løvstrøm a.k.a. Uunartoq: Interview of a Hunter from Uummannaq

*Jean-Michel Huctin*

**JMH: When you were young, how did you learn to be a hunter?**
**U:** Nobody taught me how to hunt or fish. I just learned watching my big brother.
When I was a child, if you wanted to live, you had to be a hunter. People used to hunt
sharks a lot. Hunting narwhals with kayak, not much fishing halibut like today. This
is why I know where to hunt and fish today, because I was living for hunting back then.

**JMH: What animals do you prefer to hunt today?**
**U:** I like to hunt seals on the ice. When a seal dig a hole to get on the ice, we call it
"uuttoq" which means a seal basking on the ice. When I see one like that from a far
distance, I stop my dogs and tie them to the ice. Then I slowly and silently walk and crawl,
trying to get as close as possible without being seen, hidden behind my white screen, and
without noise to be heard. Seals have very good ears. At the slightest feeling of danger,
they quickly slip into their hole back to the sea. When I'm close enough and my prey still
on the ice, I shoot it with a rifle which is tied to a small sled behind my white screen.
This is how I do it now.

**JMH: Because of trade ban in the US and Europe, seal skins products are forbidden to
export from Greenland. Most hunters are first of all fishermen, the only way for them
to make a living. What do you think about it?**
**U:** We cannot live anymore by hunting in these days because of this unfair ban. In the
past, we used to go hunting much more and I often shot a lot of seals. My wife used
to cut and dry all these seal skins to make clothing or to sell them. It was hard to prepare
seal-skins. Back then as hunters, we got paid by selling seal skins. It was nice at that
time. Since they have stopped buying seal skins, being hunter is not affordable anymore.
You can sell the meat if only someone wants it. In the summer, you have to use gas for
your boat and buy equipments, including cell-phones, GPS and marine VHF radios. It's very
expensive. And also, when there are still a lot of animals, the official quotas from the
government forbid us from hunting more. If you want to be a hunter today, it is difficult.
Even today my wife sometimes says: "I don't want to touch seal skins again!"

**JMH: Less and less people are becoming hunters today. I heard many young people
saying "I don't want to be a hunter"...**
**U:** Nowadays young people are not that interested in hunting, only a few of them.
If we compare the situation to early years, hunting was supposed to be the most important thing for the young people. It is not anymore because it is hard job, not well paid,
expensive to do... But it is our culture as Greenlanders. Some of the young people really
like hunting and keep on the tradition.

**JMH: Do you see other changes such as environmental changes? How is the sea-ice in the Uummannaq bay?**

**U:** In the past, the ice was a lot thicker. Today there are often strong winds, frequent storms, which break the ice around Uummannaq and push it away. In the spring the ice is getting thinner and softer. In 2005, there was no ice in winter and spring around Uummannaq. While in 2015, ice was very thick and stayed a long time. I heard scientists on the radio talking about the earth getting warmer. But I see that there are bad years and also good years.

**JMH: I know that polar bears rarely come into the Uummannaq bay which is not on the traditional migration route. That is why very few hunters in the whole community had the privilege of shooting one. But you did it, back in 1997. Could you tell me how you succeeded?**

**U:** One morning of 1997, I was leaving Upernavik (a town, several hundreds miles north of Uummannaq) with my dogsled. Snow had fallen down beautifully. I had 17 dogs with me, but I lost one on the way because it slipped away from the team. I stopped because I had to check the way with my binoculars from the top of an iceberg. I saw that there was something which was not a crack on ice but polar bear footprints. So I went closer to them to be sure they were really footprints. They were going to the east and I followed them. My rifle was loaded and I was so excited. One of my dogs saw the bear and followed it immediately. I cut one of the lines to let this dog run after the bear which was running away. It was fast, jumping from one bear footprint to the other. That dog is a nice dog, long and skinny. My other dogs were running while pulling the sled and I was strongly holding my rifle while sitting. The bear got closer and closer. Then it jumped and landed on one of my dogs, fortunately not harming it seriously. The dogs were trying to attack it. I suddenly realised that the bear was about to jump in my direction. Before it jumps, I shot it! The bear fell down. I got close and poked it with my gun but it was not moving anymore. I was sure that the bear was dead. I was alone and really happy. That was my first polar bear hunt!

# Inuit Qaujimajimajatuqangit

*Martin Nweeia*

*Inuit Qaujimajimajatuqangit* (IQ), "the Inuit way of knowing" is contextual with relevant environmental conditions included even in the simplest of observations. This wisdom is passed down orally through the generations, and then broadened through added experience. Its value cannot be adequately appreciated without knowing the dire consequences of life in the Arctic, which often is dependent on such knowledge. Jens Rosing, considered Greenland's Grand Old Man (Brunström, 2010), was well versed, and respected for bringing Greenland's Inuit, most notably the Inughuit and their knowledge to the forefront. As Director of Greenland's National Museum, he has explored many aspects of Inuit knowledge (Rosing, 1986), wrote and illustrated, in collaboration with the Inuit, on many of Greenland's animals including narwhals (Rosing, 1999). Recent studies of polar bears in Eastern Greenland (Escajeda et al., 2018) incorporate and demonstrate the value of Inuit knowledge showing the effects of climate change in Greenland. Hunters now were reported to hunt polar bear from boats instead of land since normal ice routes were treacherous.

Because of the interdependent communities, Inuit continually share information about their changing environment, either by radio contact concerning more immediate travel and dynamic weather conditions or later in their community meetings for more long term observations. One such observation describes the recent changes in the Arctic pack ice sheet causing normally frozen areas north of Greenland to be open twice this year for the first time.

Likewise, ice conditions in northeastern Baffin Island in 2018 have created the coolest summer in over 30 years according to hunters in Pond Inlet. As a result, there are dramatic changes and shifts in the ecosystem. Narwhals had a delayed migration of over one month as a result of pack ice sheets remaining until mid-August. Hunters from both Arctic Bay and Pond Inlet reported that their usual summering population was low and that narwhal suddenly appeared in much larger numbers further south in Clyde River. Even with these shifts, the sharing of food is integral in these communities, as a successful harvest means food for everyone in the case of narwhal mattak, skin rich in vitamins.

IQ has transformed scientific observation and results on the relationship of narwhals to their ice environment. The discovery of tusk sensory function (Nweeia et al, 2014) to salt ion gradients sheds new light on IQ from Greenlandic hunters, which has long held that narwhal are acutely aware of the weather, and particularly ice formation, that signals a migratory cue for narwhal to leave an area (Fitzhugh and Nweeia, 2017; Nweeia et al in Press).

Dramatic changes in fisheries populations have also been influenced by the increase of orcas in Greenland due to changes in ocean currents and climate change as noted by local fisherman and scientists (Lennert and Richard, 2017). Other affects of climate shifts include a rise in mercury contamination levels in Arctic biota and particularly ring seals. One cause is due to changes in sea ice extent, warming waters and air temperatures that affect the prey species available to ring seals, prey that contain higher levels of mercury (Riget et al, 2012). Thus, the ecosystem shifts in Greenland impacted by changes in climate manifest in multiple ways.

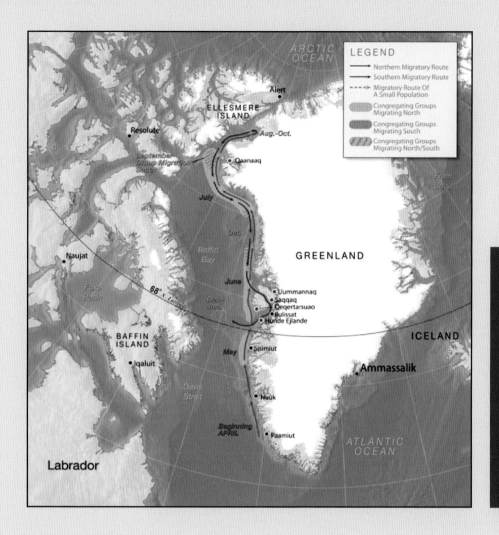

Elders in Hunde Ejland and Uummannaq described a change in narwhal migration with a two week shift in time and change around Disko Island that started in 2007.

# References

https://www.researchgate.net/profile/Rune_Dietz/publication/233418770_Temporal_trends_
        of_mercury_in_Greenland_ringed_seal_populations_in_a_warming_
        climate/links/0fcfd50aa0ac587f1b000000.pdf

https://nammco.no/wp-content/uploads/2017/08/fi08-lennert-and-richard-2017.pdf

Brunström, C.

2010. Jens Rosing: Greenland's Old Man. Royal Mail British Philatelic Bulletin, March 30.

Escajeda, E., Laidre, K.L., Born, E.W., Wiig, Ø., Atkinson, S., Dyck, M., & Lunn, N. J.

2018. Identifying shifts in maternity den phenology and habitat characteristics of polar
        bears (Ursus maritimus) in Baffin Bay and Kane Basin. Polar Biology, 41(1), 87-100.

Fitzhugh, W. and Nweeia, M.T., Eds.

2017. Narwhal: Revealing an Arctic Legend. IPI Press & Arctic Studies Center, National
        Museum of Natural History, Smithsonian Institution, Washington, D.C.

Nweeia, M.T., Eichmiller, F.C., Hauschka, P.V., Donahue, G.A., Orr, J.R., Ferguson, S.H., Watt,
        C.A. et al.

2014. Sensory ability in the narwhal tooth organ system. The Anatomical Record, 297
        (4):599-617.

Nweeia et al.

Inuit Knowledge Adds to the Discussion of Narwhal Population Dynamics, Behavior, and
        Biology. In Arctic Crashes: Peoples and Animal Relations in the Changing Arctic:
        Climate, Human or Habitat Agency in the Anthropocene. I. Krupnik, Ed. (In press)
        Smithsonian Institution Scholarly Press, Washington, DC.

Rosing, J.

1986. The sky hangs low. Penumbra Press.

Rosing, J.

1999. The Unicorn of the Arctic Sea: The Narwhal and its Habitat. (Translated by N.J. Groves).
        Penumbra Press, p. 81.

# Uummannaq—a City, a Mountain, a Symbol

*Kunuunnguaq Fleischer*

Since my childhood in Assiaat in midwest Greenland, I heard stories about the place where my father grew up and where my father's family originates, namely Uummannaq. Years passed before I settled myself in the area, first in Qaarsut, a village 23 km from Uummannaq and then in Uummannaq, where I have lived for several years.

When my then wife and I came to Uummannaq in 1974 I had spent over 10 years in Denmark, where I among other things, studied to be a teacher—and was in general greatly influenced by Danish norms and values. Being invited by my family to Uummannaq, upon arrival I was overwhelmed by the family that I had not met previously and by meeting people who I did not know but who knew my parents and therefore welcomed us "home".

The same excitement occurred when I first went from Uummannaq to Qaarsut by boat. It turned out that the skipper was my father's cousin. During the whole trip of two hours, he kept repeating: "I cannot believe that you are my cousin's son, welcome, welcome, welcome". This warmth and immediacy proved to be the hallmark of all the people through the years with whom I came to associate with and love through joys and sorrows.

In 1974 Qaarsut was still characteristically a seal hunting settlement, although there was some halibut fishing. Seal skin was the sought commodity, followed by narwhals and beluga, an occassional minke, various sea birds and lots of grouse and hares from the mountains which rose up behind the settlement of Qaarsut.

One of our new colleagues was from Switzerland, who in addition to English and his native German also spoke Danish and Greenlandic. Being fully integrated into the community, he joined in hunting and fishing trips. And, he would cruise around in his open boat, with sails flying and drove a snowmobile in winter. I mention him because he was in many ways a picture of how the Inuit have always been able to adapt and accept differences and changes. Differences in culture, values and norms, and in general the intangible culture as well as changes in climate and the material culture.

Just as our colleague adapted to life in Qaarsut, the people of Qaarsut learned much from him—as the Inuit have done for thousands of years. During my time in Qaarsut, its people collectivly learned to hunt seals from a Norwegian built boat with a Finnish rifle, shooting American cartridges while they heard the news from a Japanese radio and drank coffee from Brazil.

I have lived in Uummannaq several times, the last time from 2003 to 2007. Compared to the first time that I came to Uummannaq in the 1970s, there were noticeable changes in the climate, for example, there was a winter where there was no sea ice so fishermen could not fish from the ice. There were not as many dogs back in town. The sun came a day earlier in spring, because the glacier on the Nuussuaq peninsula where the sun came out in the spring, had melted so much that we could watch the sun set over the glacier earlier than usual.

But although both the climate, the political conditions and many other things have changed, men are still the same: warm-hearted and welcoming. Uummannaq, which means heart mountain, is not only the name of the city, the area and the mountains, but also a powerful symbol of the entire Greenland soul.

# Lindsay: Teaching in Qaarsut, Greenland

**On language**

Greenlandic is a synthetic language, which results in very long words. A plane could complete its flight before you understand to "put table in upright position." Greenlandic language is double daunting. It sounds as when composing a noun all adjective attributes come before the noun, which is last...All words have to be planed ahead, which for an outsider could very well take an entire day. Much of pronunciation involves sounding with breath in and out. (See Veerle Van Geenhoven. *Semantic Incorporation and Indefinite Descriptions: Semantic and Syntactic Aspects of Noun Incorporation in West Greenlandic.* Dissertations in Linguistics. Stanford, California: CSLI Publications. 1995.)

Greenland is an oral culture, enjoying talk and laughter. As Kunuunnguaq Fleischer said: "Eskimo is special," leaving his comments at that.

**Conversation with educator Kunuunnguaq Fleischer**

Postcolonial flashes by Kunuunnguaq: What does a European-type education mean in Greenland? What is good education in settlements? 50% drop out in 2005 and go back to settlements to fish. Then, what happens if cut back by regulations or fishery collapses?

What do children need to know of life beyond settlements? How does discourse go regarding education in community with elders, with the parents? With the children? What do you do with mentally or physically handicapped children? I admire Kunuunnguaq for not giving up, being depressed or overwhelmed.

**On teaching in the settlement of Qaarsut**

This morning I teach English. The 7 eleven-year olds are just great, responsive. Lukas, a small 11 year old, with a skeptical expression and turned-down mouth, has father who manages local skin shop. His mother is an aide at the old people's home.

Did my thing on where I lived, my home—drawing on board. Emphasized Georgetown (Maine) fishermen to make connection with their families, also drew lobster—green and red—where I worked and our house.

These teen girls are not the easiest. First, we talked a little about them – name, parents, names and ages and siblings' names and ages, pointing out concepts of 'oldest,' 'youngest,' 'in between.' They then asked about me—full name, age, where I live. Headmaster Esben Christiansen got out the atlas and globe to place people.

After class, girls returned to teach me Greenlandic. Whatever I say, a joke on me, of course. But, I could watch closely their biology of speech. Tongue moves in ways other than in our language. One, tongue is curled, tip against front teeth—hence curled so air and sound have to go around side of tongue—damn near impossible to do! They laughed, and I said "bye."

Friday August 26—the school's 'blueberry day' and a day of field botany study. Preparation for the 'great excursion' begins with teachers preparing students with talks about plants, parts of plants, sites.

Plastic bags carried by students are filled with mosses, small willow branches and mix of blueberries and crowberries, even Labrador tea.

Big event—Hansi, one of the teachers, found in a pool of water, several small animals in a shallow pool near mountaintop. How do plants and animal survive the brutal winter?

Later, that evening, I went by myself to photograph places in town to make board game for school using nouns and verbs.

**On difficulties of teaching in Qaarsut—some selected thoughts, 2005**

- I love the school!
- Overwhelming oral culture and TV
- No sense where future is except fishing
- No sense what future means
- Unusual talented children with little to no support
- How does government policy recognize this situation—Greenland and Denmark?
- No way—given cultural factors—can education be at Danish level.
- Children learn three languages—Greenlandic, Danish, English.
- One factor is learning how to be in classroom so that one can learn a subject there.
- The children themselves: really lively, responsive except if no sleep, shy, intimidated in some way—myself included, as an outsider, and care about each one.

# INDEX

# Additional Image Credits

**Photographs of cultural objects at beginning of each chapter, as well as at the end of Chapter 5 and Chapter 7, are photographs either taken in the field or from the collection of the author.**

The beginnings of the cultural objects represented here did not start with me. My wife Lindsay with her then husband had started the collection in Canada in the late 1970's.

The collection continued with objects I amassed as I found my way to Greenland over three decades of travel, beginning from just across the Maine border to Maritime Canada, Quebec, Maritime Canada, Newfoundland and Labrador, Nunavut, Alaska, Iceland and Greenland.

Their inclusion here represents my journey of discovery.

**Postscript:**
 **Lindsay Crittenden Dorney-Richard**

On January 21, 2001, after a month in Antarctica, we set sail on the Russian ship *Marya Yermolova* from Livingston, a small island, located just to the north of the Antarctic Peninsula that juts towards the southern-most point of South America. In between is the 350 mile wide Drake Passage, where the turbulent waters of the Pacific surge eastward into the south Atlantic, requiring us to take fifteen hours to cross. Our ship then maneuvered northwest through the Beagle Channel to Tierra del Fuego, Chile and that region's central place, Ushuaia, on January 23, to begin a series of flights to Boston. (From Lindsay's Field Notes, January 2001.)

# Contributors

## Ann Andreasen

Family psychotherapist, Ann is director of the Uummannaq Children's home and director/cofounder of the Uummannaq Polar Institute. She is also producer of a number of international films, including the awarded feature film "Inuk" (2012). For her many years educational achievement with youth, she has won many prestigious prizes, including the *Nersornaat* in silver awarded by the Greenlandic parliament.

## Esben Skytte Christiansen

Esben, MA & BA, was born 1949 in Copenhagen, Denmark. Educated in History of Art, History, Philosophy, Romance and Slavonic Languages, and Social Sciences at universities and other higher education institutions in several countries (Denmark, Sweden, France, Italy, Spain, Mexico, Cuba, GDR, CSSR, UK, USSR), 1966-85.

He has been a teacher of languages, history, social sciences at higher education institutions, grammar schools and secondary schools in Denmark, Australia, Japan, Mongolia, Argentina, Chile, USSR, GDR, Latvia, Kazakhstan, Armenia, UK, France, Morocco, Tunisia, Tanzania, South Africa, Greenland since 1972.

He has served as interpreter and translator for publishing houses, cultural and international societies, exhibition institutions, national state authorities, international private firms, and the Danish Royal House, 1986-1999. Other professional endeavours have included National NGO-coordinator of participant activities and negotiations at the UN supported International Peace Congress in Copenhagen 1986 (*UN International Year of Peace*), at the CSCE-meetings in Paris 1989, Copenhagen 1990 and Moscow 1991 (*Conference on Security and Cooperation in Europe*), at the International Social Summit in Copenhagen 1995.

From 1992–2002, he was an international election observer in SNG-countries and Mongolia. From 1986–1996, he was secretary and international courier / envoy of two private foundations with a view of supporting museum and cultural activities, UN and peace caring purposes respectively, 1986-1996.

He then turned to primary school teaching in west Greenland as teacher and principal at the schools of Saattut and Qaarsut, villages in the Uummannaq district 2002–2007. In 2012, he began duties in east Greenland in Tasiilaq, working as a teacher and deputy head, responsible for EU-financed educational exchange programs where he continues. Esben is a renowned scholar of Hans Christian Andersen.

## William W. Fitzhugh

William W. Fitzhugh is Arctic Curator and Director of the Smithsonian Institution's Arctic Studies Center in the National Museum of Natural History in Washington, D.C. and Visiting Professor at Dartmouth College. He has conducted anthropological and archaeological research throughout the circumpolar north. The narwhal exhibition and book is the latest in a series of Smithsonian exhibitions that include Bering Sea Eskimos, the Ainu of Japan, cultures of Siberia and Alaska, Vikings, Genghis Khan, and ancient Bering Sea Eskimo art. His most recent books are *Maine to Greenland: Exploring the Maritime Far Northeast* and *Bark and Skin Boats of Northern Eurasia*, to appear in 2019.

## Kunuunnguaq Fleischer

Born and raised in Assiaat, Greenland, Kunuunnguaq was educated in Denmark. He was teacher and head of the municipal schools in Uummannaq. He is now retired and living in Denmark with his wife Naja who was principal in Edvard Kruse-p Atuarfia (the primary school in Uummannaq). Elsewhere in Nuuk and Denmark, Kunuunnguaq has served as researcher, consultant, administrator and linguist.

## Jean-Michel Huctin

An anthropologist at the University of Versailles Saint-Quentin-en-Yvelines, France, Jean-Michel is co-founder of the Uummannaq Polar Institute, Greenland. His PhD was on anthropology of Uummannaq and the Children's Home where he has been periodically working during the last 18 years, including co-writing and co-producing the feature film "Inuk" (2012). He co-edited in French the international science book *Greenland. Climate, Ecology, Society* (2016).

## Jakob Løvstrom (Unartoq)

Jakob Løvstrøm is well known in Uummannaq by his nickname 'Unartoq' which means, "hot" or "burning". It is true that he has a warm and lively personality, with a great sense of humor. As an elder (he is 75) and a great musher who still has a very fast dog team, he is well respected not only in the settlement where he lives but also in all the Uummannaq community. Although he carries on professional fishing, he remains a hunter in his soul and for sure one of the best in the region. Every winter and spring for the last twenty years, he has been very keen on working with the Uummannaq Children's Home where all the kids love him, especially by transporting, guiding and teaching youth during month-long dogsled expeditions on the ice. His professional skills and educational talent as well as his old Eskimo-like charisma has convinced a lot of foreign filmmakers to ask him to be a main character in many documentaries and in one feature when he tells about his life as a hunter, including when he shot a polar bear in a special way.

## Martin T. Nweeia

Martin T. Nweeia is Lecturer at the Harvard School of Dental Medicine and clinical assistant professor at Case Western Reserve University School of Dental Medicine where he received his doctorates of dental surgery and medicine. He is content curator for the exhibit *Narwhal: Revealing an Arctic Legend* and a research associate in the Marine Mammal Program at the Smithsonian Institution where he previously received fellowships in physical anthropology and vertebrate zoology. As a National Science Foundation scientist, he is principal investigator for Narwhal Tusk Discoveries, the Narwhal Genome Initiative, and Narwhal HoloLens. Martin has conducted 17 field expeditions, most recently supported by the Prince Albert II Foundation and given the Lowell Thomas Award from the Explorers Club.

## Erik Torm

Erik is a former headmaster and school innovator. He has worked with non-profit school projects and cultural projects in Denmark, Slovakia and Greenland. At present time, he is Project Advisor at Uummannaq Polar Institute. Over the years, he has authored educational literature in Denmark. Erik is a Uummannaq Polar Institute Research Fellow.

# The Author

Wilfred E. Richard is a Research Associate with the Arctic Studies Center, Smithsonian National Museum of Natural History, Washington, D.C., and a Research Fellow with the Uummannaq Polar Institute in Greenland. He served as a Mellon Environmental Fellow in Residence at Bates College, Lewiston, Maine. Academic credentials include a PhD in Geography with the Faculty of Environmental Studies, University of Waterloo, Ontario, Canada, and a MA in Economic Anthropology, University of Massachusetts, Amherst, Massachusetts. He served with the U.S. Marine Corps in east and southeast Asia. Will makes his home in the coastal woods of Georgetown, Maine.

Since his early teen years, Will has been a lover of the woods, backpacking from the White Mountains of New Hampshire to the Appalachians of Maritime Canada where he was one of the founding members of the International Appalachian Trail. To his hiking, he added sea kayaking, becoming a Registered Maine Guide. With Bill Fitzhugh he worked on an archaeological dig on Québec's Lower North Shore for 12 years.

With co-author, William Fitzhugh, they produced *Maine to Greenland—Exploring the Maritime Far Northeast*. Washington DC: Smithsonian Books. 2014.

It is a commonplace of all religious thought,

even the most primitive, that the man seeking vision

and insight must go apart from his fellows

and live for a time in the wilderness. If he is of the

proper sort, he will return with a message

from the god he set out to seek, but even if he

has failed in that particular, he will have

had a vision or seen a marvel, and these are always

worth listening to and thinking about.

— *Loren Eiseley. The Immense Journey (1957 [1946], 163).*